W9-CBU-922

ROAR OF THE CANON:

Kott and Marowitz on Shakespeare

by

CHARLES MAROWITZ

Roar of the Canon: Kott and Marowitz on Shakespeare
by Charles Marowitz

ISBN 1-55783-474-1

Library of Congress Cataloging-in-Publication Data:

Marowitz, Charles
Roar of the Canon: Kott and Marowitz on Shakespeare / by Charles Marowitz
p. cm.
ISBN 1-55783-474-1
1. Shakespeare, William, 1564-1616 -- Criticism and interpretation.
2. Shakespeare, William, 1564-1616--Dramatic production. I. Marowitz, Charles. II. Title.

PR2976 .K68 2001
822.3'3--dc21

2001045130

APPLAUSE THEATRE & CINEMA BOOKS
151 W46th Street, 8th Floor
New York, NY 10036
Phone: (212) 575-9265
Fax: (646) 562-5852
email: info@applausepub.com
www.applausepub.com

COMBINED BOOK SERVICES LTD.
Units I/K, Paddock Wood Distribution Centre
Paddock Wood, Tonbridge,
Kent TN 12 6UU
Phone: (44) 01892 837171
Fax: (44) 01892 837272

SALES & DISTRIBUTION, HAL LEONARD CORP.
7777 West Bluemound Road, P.O. Box 13819
Milwaukee, WI 53213
Phone: (414) 774-3630 Fax: (414) 774-3259
email:halinfo@halleonard.com
internet: www.halleonard.com

BY THE SAME AUTHOR

[Books & Collections]

STAGE DUST	(Scarecrow Press)
THE OTHER WAY	(Applause Books)
ALARUMS & EXCURSIONS	(Applause Books)
RECYCLING SHAKESPEARE	(Macmillan)
DIRECTING THE ACTION	(Applause)
BURNT BRIDGES	(Hodder & Stoughton)
PROSPERO'S STAFF	(Indiana Univ. Press)
POTBOILERS	(Marion Boyars, Inc.)
CLEVER DICK	(Dramatists Play Svc.)
SEX WARS	(Marion Boyars, Inc.)
THE ACT OF BEING	(Taplinger Press)
THE MAROWITZ SHAKESPEARE	(Marion Boyars)
CONFESSIONS OF A COUNTERFEIT CRITIC	(Eyre-Methuen)
THE METHOD AS MEANS	(Barrie & Rockliffe)

[Plays & Translations]

QUACK	(Dramatists Play Svc.)
BOULEVARD COMEDIES	(Smith & Kraus)
STAGE FRIGHT	(Dramatists Play Svc.)
BASHVILLE IN LOVE	(Samuel French, Ltd.)
SHERLOCK'S LAST CASE	(Dramatists Play Svc.)
CLEVER DICK	(Dramatists Play Svc.)
WILDE WEST	(Dramatists Play Svc.)
DISCIPLES	(Dramatists Play Svc.)
HEDDA	(Aschehoug, Nwy.)
ARTAUD AT RODEZ	(Marion Boyars, Inc.)
THE SHREW	(Marion Boyars, Inc.)
MEASURE FOR MEASURE	(Marion Boyars, Inc.)
AN OTHELLO	(Penguin Books)
A MACBETH	(Marion Boyars, Inc.)
VARIATIONS ON THE MERCHANT OF VENICE	(Marion Boyars, Inc.)
THE CRITIC AS ARTIST	(Hansom Books)
THE MAROWITZ HAMLET & TRAGICAL HISTORY OF DR. FAUSTUS	(Penguin Books)
CYRANO DE BERGERAC	(Smith & Kraus)
MAKBETT	(Grove Press)
AND THEY PUT HANDCUFFS ON THE FLOWERS	(Grove Press)

for Jane,

CONTENTS

INTRODUCTION

By Charles Marowitz

There is a certain kind of critic who, transcending the formal confines of criticism, sometimes spills over into philosophy. Goethe was such a critic so, in a very different way, was Samuel Johnson and, after him, Matthew Arnold. Scrutinizing art, which is a finely-filtered composite of life-experiences, cannot help but cast the mind upward from the work of artists into universal truths or falsehoods from which those experiences have been hewn, and so the natural tendency of all criticism, good or bad, is an evaluation of the ideas or ideologies that condition the way we live.

It is a truism in the theatre that the more life-experience an actor accumulates the greater the emotional reserves he or she has to draw on. At base, all art is a reproduction of an artist's experience, no matter how far-fetched its formal disguises may be. In criticism, there are far less disguises, and those that exist are far more transparent. You may not be able to track down the intellectual substructure that underpins a Shakespeare or a Dickens but the ideas that condition the work of an A.C. Bradley or a T.S. Eliot will be fairly discernible.

Jan Kott is one of the few critics whose work overlaps the analysis and exegesis we normally associate with Shakespearean criticism. It's not so much that he is more incisive or more profound than other critics but that his frame of reference stretches beyond the circumference around which the Canon is usually wrapped. When Kott writes about civil strife in Romeo and Juliet's Verona, you get intimations of war-torn Europe, of young people trapped in regional conflicts that supercede family disputes. Kott's eye, like the telescope it is, extends or retracts depending on the vantage-point from which the critic considers fictional events. He is constantly reading the changes in characters' fortunes according to the fluctuations of his personal barometer, one which has experienced such drastic highs and lows, there is virtually no conflict in the canon which does not automatically trigger some concomitant memory in the critic. When Barnadine in "Measure For Measure" is temporarily reprieved from death because he is in no fit state to be hanged, it immediately echoes Kott's own scheduled execution in Nazi-occupied Poland from which he was spared because he too was in no fit state to have his life terminated. When a Bolingbroke or a Kent is banished, it triggers a flood of memory from Kott's wanderings in Eastern Europe when he was obliged to flee from one country to another to escape the Wehrmacht death squads or avoid a political putsch. His several brushes with death have given Kott a percipience about life that is denied the critic whose greatest calamity is breaking down on the freeway or discovering he has been denied tenure.

* * *

After the publication of SHAKESPEARE OUR CONTEMPORARY in 1964, Kott's influence began to be felt in theatres throughout Europe; in the work of Georgio Strehler at the Teatro Piccolo, Ariane Mnouchkine at the Theatre du Soleil and perhaps most noticeably in the work of Peter Brook and other directors at the Royal Shakespeare Company. "I read his writing with passionate interest," wrote Peter Brook "and at the time of preparing "King Lear" it took just one phrase, one image amongst so many, to open a thousand doors. Gloucester hurls himself in despair off a cliff and in his mind his act is totally real; for the audience it is just an actor making an absurd little jump on a bare stage. The theatre allows us to enter into a passionately held belief and exposes us its absurdity. This is the typical Kott pebble thrown in the pond where the ripples spread and spread, helping us to see the relativity of apparently unshakeable convictions."

Kott's perceptions, filtered through Brook's scenic imagination, made LEAR the perfect union of critical insight and theatrical evocation. But it also opened the door for an onslaught of garishly 'relevant' Shakespearean productions in which contemporary parallels, like glaring foundation garments, were worn over rather than under outward attire. Many directors, misreading Kott, began to see Shakespeare as a billboard onto which they could plaster topical newspaper clippings or arbitrary notions of recent historical events. John Elsom, the English critic, described a singularly embarrassing instance of this which took place at the International Association of Theatre Critics at the Young Vic in 1986.

Kott, whose Polish-English diction is sometimes hard to follow, was suddenly assisted by Michgael Bogdonov, an English director who "in coming to (Kott's) rescue" writes Elsom "fell into every trap that Kott had been anxious to avoid. 'I look for my inspiration for the day's rehearsals,' Bogdanov said 'and for what the plays mean in the headlines of the morning's papers.' He went on to give examples and Kott seemed to freeze into a polite panic, smiling through. 'When Prince John meets the Archbishop on neutral ground, and tricks the rebels into laying down their weapons', Bogdanov remarked, 'I think of Reagan and Gorbachev in Reykjavik.' When Henry V invaded France, he thought of Margaret Thatcher and the Falklands War, of both of which he disapproved; and Kott who must have lived through more dodgy pacts, military escapades, and armed peace initiatives than Bogdanov had had first nights, leant forward, hand cupped to ear, like Nelson with a telescope to his blind eye, and nodded with Polish inscrutability."

Kott's contemporaneity is always contained within a Shakespearean vessel. The notion of daubing modern parallels onto the plays is, for him, tantamount to applying graffiti to the Parthenon. "Hamlet," Kott wrote, "is like a sponge. Unless produced in a stylized or antiquarian fashion, it immediately absorbs all the problems of our time." In the same essay, Elson points out "(Kott) warned against trying to present Hamlet as a left-bank student existentialist or in a similar trendy garb. 'What I have in mind is not a forced topicality. (wrote Kott) 'What matters is that through Shakespeare's text we ought to get at our modern experience, anxiety and sensibility.' "

The key-phrase here is 'through Shakespeare's text' which doesn't necessarily mean preserving every element of its literal purity but *does* mean immersing oneself in the nuances and endless potentialities that the text offers. Like an arithmetical equation, the sum a director arrives at needs to be 'proven' by reference back to the original figures. That doesn't necessarily mean that two and two must always make four, but it does mean that one must separate apples from oranges, concepts from aberrations, insights from delusions.

Exasperation is often expressed at directors' tendencies to 're-think' and then re-jig the classics. It is the most obstreperous complaint of the Bardoltrous traditionalists. If one recoils from crass 'reinterpretations' of Shakespeare set in post-nuclear wastelands ("Macbeth") or the world of Iran-Contra ("Coriolanus") or Caribbean islands dominated by colonialist exploiters ("The Tempest") or a fascist, Mosleyite Britain in the Thirties ("Richard III"), it is fair to ask what kind of parallels *are* acceptable? If certain productions go too far and others not far enough, what precisely are the permissible boundaries of classical reinterpretation?

Before attempting to answer that one, I would remind readers of Jean Anouilh's "Antigone", presented in Paris in 1943 at the height of the German occupation; a production in which the conflict between an authoritarian bureaucracy and a free-spirited rebel stirred every Frenchman who saw it. Its sub-text, resistance to the Petain government and the Nazis that installed it, spoke loud and clear to The French public. The 'parallel' was in the society and therefore in that society's collective consciousness. Euripide's story was played straight (had it been explicitly slanted against the Germans, it would never have been allowed) and yet the original work coalesced with the bitterness of Frenchmen who loathed the enemy that had invaded their land. Something of the same effect was created by the Rushtaveli production of "Richard III" in Georgia, Russia where the figure of a bloodthirsty monarch unmistakably evoked the specter of Joseph Stalin in a land still very much under the thumb of the Soviets. The classic and the temper-of-the-times subtly combined to produce new subject matter for its audience - without revision or alteration of the original works.

In those instances, there was a proclivity on the part of the play and an attitude on the part of its performers that established a *natural* parallel. The silent collaborator here was the audience and they were interpreting the ancient fable in terms of their modern sensibility; Shakespeare and Euripides addressing contemporary concerns were, in a very palpable sense, their contemporaries.

The answer to the question previously posed on the subject of interpretive limits is that no parameters can be laid down and no formulae agreed. But if there is an issue in the times that speak to a resonance in the play, a line of communication is automatically opened. The determining factor, as Kott suggests, has to do with selecting the appropriate classic work that inherently contains the topical message. The choice alone is sometimes sufficient for bringing Shakespeare 'up to date' and without the anachronistic interpolations which directors find impossible to resist.

This I believe is what Kott had in mind when he spoke of the marriage of historicity and contemporaneity. It has virtually nothing to do with letting Shakespeare 'speak for himself' because in every instance, a director or a company-of-actors are inflecting Shakespeare's words towards a message the playwright, living in another age, was incapable of imagining.

But contemporary relevance to one side, it needs to be pointed out that there are certain humanistic truths embedded in the canon that are as pertinent today as they were when these plays were first written; a certain quantum of universality which needs neither embellishment nor slanting in order to speak to modern audiences, and in those instances, we are forcibly reminded of Ben Jonson's judgement that "He was not of an age but for all time." But perhaps the construction to be put on that Jonsonian compliment is that there is so much mutability in Shakespeare's works that he can be rethought and reconstituted from age to age, as indeed he has been since the end of the 17th century.

* * *

Kott's influence with a wide variety of stage-directors (in addition to Brook's "LEAR" at the RSC, he also contributed to Clifford Williams all-male version of AS YOU LIKE IT) infers a certain utilitarian aspect to Shakespearean criticism which is hard to find among comparable critics. Olivier based certain aspects of his HAMLET interpretation on the texts of the analyst and Freud-biographer, Ernest Jones. When Peter Hall was director of The

PAUL SCOFIELD *in the storm scene from Peter Brook's Royal Shakespeare Production of* KING LEAR, *heavily influenced by Jan Kott's essay* KING LEAR or END GAME.

Photo credit: *The Shakespeare Centre Library.*

National Theatre in London, he applied some of John Russell Brown's ideas about 'hands-off' direction which that critic had proselytized in his treatise, "Free Shakespeare". But it is hard to cite a Shakespearean critic other than Kott who has left an indelible mark on contemporary productions. Directors are always cribbing ideas from a variety of scholars and critics, but only in Kott's case is one able to trace a direct genealogical line between a critical concept and a finished production.

And yet if criticism is to be of any practical use to the theatre on which it is a merciless parasite, critics *ought* to exert influence on stage-directors and directors *ought to* seek out critics to help qualify, shape and infiltrate the ideas they pass on to actors. In theory, this is the job of the Dramaturg or Literary Manager but in reality, the people who hold those positions are often aggrandized play-readers or go-betweens for writers and managements. Unfortunately, the prejudice against the scholar-critic runs deep in the professional theatre and the best way to eliminate it is for criticism to come up with interesting 'playable values' rather than theoretical *apercus* which merely tickle the cerebral cortex and then get diluted in the bloodstream. There are such things as literary perceptions which are dazzlingly original but cannot be translated into theatrical terms. Harold Bloom is perhaps the best example of this. But there is also a kind of criticism that forces radical reassessments of commonly-held beliefs whose effects can be read in the work of actors and designers and which intrinsically belong to the theatre rather than to the text-book. We rely on directorial imagination to suffuse the works of William Shakespeare and either look forward to, or recoil from, the innovations of highly inventive men and women as they impose their novel interpretations on the Comedies, Histories and Tragedies. But Kott demonstrates that there is much that can be learned from astute criticism and probing scholarship, and that a combination of those virtues, filtered through the practical talents of gifted directors, can open new vistas in the theatre. The stage-director is so seduced by 'effects' — unexpected period settings, contradictory character-choices, startling mixtures of race and gender — that he often neglects the efficacy that comes from a penetrating reassessment of the fundamental material itself; the soil, stone and plant-life of the plays themselves. Here, critics like Kott can provide a real service — nor would it in any way usurp the director's traditional role. A good idea, whether it comes from an actor or a critic, is just the first stage of the artifact that the director must conjure into being using the tools of the theatre. It is a partnership that seems so obvious and mutually enriching, and yet one that many in the professional theatre seem to abominate.

* * *

In *Wrestling With Jan Kott*, I allude to the way in which Jan made a connection between Female Mud Wrestling and early English bearbaiting. John Elsom describes yet another instance of the improvisational flexibility of Jan's mind. Walking through Covent Garden at the end of a theatre-conference, Elson writes: "There were some kids playing football in an alley. Jan Kott, in his seventies with a history of serious heart attacks, joined in. He couldn't stop himself. The ball was there and it had to be kicked. When he failed to score, his look of disappointment was palpable. One of the boys passed the ball back to him and this time he got a little closer to the goal. Satisfied, he walked on to his hotel speculating idly about whether Eliza Doolittle or her father would approve of what had happened to Covent Garden, an act of market gentrification. Kott called it (if I remember correctly) the curse of Pygmalion."

Kott, like a centipede, stands with one foot in the 20th century, another in the Renaissance, yet another in Attica, one more in the Restoration, and still others in periods from the middle-ages to modernism, and like the centipede, all those tentacles move together in astonishing coordination. He has the mind of a seasoned time-traveler who, at the flick of a neuron, can make a connection between past, present and future. Paradoxically, it is his researches into the archival past that sweep him inexorably into contemporary discoveries. His war-time experiences, first under the Nazis and then the Soviet occupation of Poland, have given him a favorable vantage point from which to view the intrigues and assassinations that constantly occur in Shakespeare. I doubt that any scandal, atrocity or devastation in the canon doesn't conjure up some parallel experience from his own life. "Kott" as Peter Brook pointed out "is undoubtedly the only writer on Elizabethan matters who assumes without question that everyone of his readers will at some point or other have been woken up by the police in the middle of the night."

It is this 'living in the real world' which has enabled him to see through the literary conventions that often hamstring other critics. For a typical classical scholar, a nuance is a connection made between one work of art and another; for Kott it is a perceptive flash which reveals the similarity between a fictive incident and the factual reality of which it is only a shard. It is a facility which, when extrapolated, puts almost all of Shakespearean scholarship into question. Should critics be investigating literary contexts, historical antecedents, stylistic resemblances, and the interplay of words and ideas? Or should the critic approach art the way the analyst does the patient's psyche — trying to make connections between past experience and present behavior? Should one experience Shakespeare as an encounter between a modern and a Renaissance sensibility and go in search of common ground, or ingest Shakespeare like a medicinal fluid to see how it begins to work on our nervous system and affects our minds? When Kott calls Shakespeare his contemporary, he is being equivocal because we know as little about our own time as we do Shakespeare's. "Even if everyone else believes that he is inevitably a contemporary of the period in which he lives," writes Peter Brook "it is not true. There are very few who live their time." If that is the case then are we not imposing our contemporary confusion onto Shakespeare's, and could it be that the 'parallels' we are constantly discovering are simply echoes of our own ambiguity, our own deeply-rooted uncertainty, our own inability to define moral absolutes? Could it be that the real appeal of Shakespeare, what makes him both modern and 'relevant', is that he has anticipated the chaos and confusion which are the hallmark of modern times and that, when one comes right down to it, he has as few answers as we do.

Troubling speculations like these are the natural spin-offs of exposure to Kott's mind. I would say that, at base, he brings a kind of debilitating cynicism to the study of Shakespeare, were it not for the fact that his darkest and most disturbing insights fire up trains-of-thought that make us reevaluate received wisdom — both about Shakespeare and our own lives — and it is that which ultimately leads us to enlightening reappraisals of both. With Kott every dark, labyrinthine journey ends on the top of a high hill and the splendor of a fresh vista.

The centerpiece of this book is the dialogues between Jan Kott and myself, but it also contains monologues; that is, lectures, articles and musings of my own with which Kott might quite violently disagree. That's okay. We have disagreed in the past and those differences-of-opinion have usually been more stimulating than falling into a lock-step with like-minded individuals. I mention this because I wouldn't want anyone to think that Kott subscribes to all the ideas expressed in the non-Kottish parts of this book.

Kott is a scholar, an academic and a highly erudite man of letters; I, a director, reviewer and sometime-playwright. We are obliged to approach Shakespeare differently and with different objectives. Much of what I write about has come directly from theatrical experience and the speculations that underlie practical work with actors. Much of Kott's ideas come from a breadth of classical knowledge and canny intuitions about life and art which then seeped into the minds of directors from many countries, and subsequently found their way onto the stage. They seeped into my mind as well and, like all intellectual influences, often got radically transformed, assuming shapes that their progenitor would neither recognize nor endorse. That's the nature of an influence; like a protein it comes from without, gets ingested and then assimilated into one's own bloodstream.

Anyone looking for unity between one chapter of this book and the other will be frustrated. Hopefully, the notions of a Shakespearean critic and a director dealing with classics will supplement each other but they may, just as likely, be at odds. The object is not so much symbiosis as it is bi-partite diagnosis, proceeding from differing standpoints and different sets of priorities. With Shakespeare, no examination is ever definitive. It is all 'second opinions' and, as with the medical profession, they are divided, contradictory and sometimes outrageous.

Charles Marowitz

PREFACE

by Robert Brustein

In his introduction, Charles Marowitz has done us the great service of reintroducing to public awareness one of the seminal critical minds of the twentieth century. It has been almost half a century since Jan Kott first published Shakespeare Our Contemporary and totally exploded our thinking about how Shakespeare could be produced on stage. But his capacity to urge contemporary parallels on the classics, not through specious updating so much as through lived experience, has remained as fresh and inspiring as when he first produced that groundbreaking book.

Kott opened new vistas for hundreds of classical directors, including Marowitz himself, not only with his work on Shakespeare but with his later insights into the Greeks. To him, every great playwright was our contemporary, and it was our obligation in the theatre to make their plays as startling and unpredictable as on the day they were written. Artaud's battle cry, "No More Masterpieces" might very well have been Kott's. But whereas Artaud wanted to return the theatre to a ritual of blood and instinct, Kott continually tried to refresh great drama through deeper imagination and more vital scholarship.

We have all been the beneficiaries of his incisive, profound, and original thinking. To speak personally, Kott had an immense influence on our work at Yale during the year he was in residence there in the mid-sixties, an inspiration that continued not only at the Yale Repertory Theatre but at the American Repertory Theatre as well. Charles Marowitz has emphasized Kott's impact on the British stage, to which Marowitz was a practicing witness. But there are scores of European, American, and Irish directors — Andrei Serban, Robert Woodruff, Marco Martinelli, Declan Donnellan, Ariane Mnouchkine, Yuri Yuremin, Elizabeth LeCompte, Des MacAnuff, Adrian Hall, Bob McGrath, Francois Rochaix, Marcus

Stern (the list is too long to conclude) — who owe a creative debt to Kott's unique work.

The twentieth century has often been called the century of the director. What is often overlooked is that it was also the century of the classical playwright, in that a host of neglected or overlooked plays of the past were brought to public attention by interpretive artists under Kott's influence. Jan Kott led the way in bringing adventurous intellectual insights to truthful, concrete, and therefore original readings of classical plays. In that sense, all of us interested in a more penetrating, more serious theatre have had the occasion to admire and imitate Jan Kott. Yes, and to wrestle with and be pinned to the mat by him as well.

TRANSLATOR'S NOTE

The dialogues with Jan Kott were tape-recorded over a period of several months during the mid-80s and early 90s when the critic was resident in Santa Monica, California. Jan speaks what is best described as non-syntactical, Slavic-styled, broken English and, to a certain extent, I was obliged to 'translate' his words into their English equivalent. This was no easy task and in several places, knowing what he was meaning to say but not quite saying it, I have come to his aid with words of my own which I believe convey his intention. In transcribing these talks, I have tried to retain his simple, tentative, unadorned, sometimes blunt use of the English language but wherever I felt I could refine a phrase to better illuminate his sense, I have done so. The italicized questions are, of course mine; the replies, his.

WRESTLING

WITH

JAN KOTT

The beefy brunette, her skin glistening with Crisco cooking-oil, held the brawny blonde in an impregnable hammerlock. After a couple of perfunctory twists, the blonde was supine and the brunette, now astride her stomach, began pulling out her hair. The crowd, mostly raucous college-boys and beer-swilling regulars, cheered and whistled as the triumphant brunette, imitating the action of a piston, pounced heavily on the blonde's abdomen. In a moment, two other female contenders drenched in mud would begin the main event of the evening.

At a ringside table in the Hollywood Tropicana Club, the sleazy Mecca of female mud wrestling in Los Angeles, I sat with Professor Jan Kott, recipient of the George Jean Nathan Award for drama criticism and arguably, one of the most fecund Shakespearean scholars of his day. Kott, recently arrived in Los Angeles and having declined previous invitations to theatres and concerts, had asked me to arrange tickets for the mud-wrestling and was clearly fascinated by the ritual of men paying for the privilege of massaging female combatants before they laid into each other in the makeshift ring.

When we left the club, he coolly elucidated the qualities of the evening, clearly impressed by the intense order of the highly-structured social situation: men sheepishly keeping their hands at their sides while bikini-clad Amazons, in return for cash, planted hot, sweaty kisses onto their lips and muscular bodyguards hovered over them making sure erotic stimuli never gave way to tactile contact.

"It's very much like Elizabethan bear-baiting," said Kott. "An atmosphere of abandon and sexual aggression but firmly suppressed and performed strictly according to the rules."

If one knew Jan Kott, it would be no surprise that of all the entertainments offered in Los Angeles, he would choose the incorrigible art of Female Mud Wrestling. In Scotland where I first met him, he claimed to have found the origins of medieval tavern-theatre in an Edinburgh pub.

*   *   *

Are there particular plays of Shakespeare which, for one reason or another, become relevant at particular times in history, and if so, which ones are particularly relevant today?

To my mind, all of Shakespeare's plays — or almost all — are relevant, but at certain times, some works become more contemporary than others do. Take HAMLET, for instance, a play which has been popular for many generations but which, in the Romantic period, took on an increased popularity in Europe. The other striking example would be TROILUS AND CRESSIDA; a play which had been performed very rarely in England up until the start of the second world war. During the Munich period, when Chamberlain signed the non-aggression pact with Hitler, TROILUS AND CRESSIDA became, for the young people and for the intelligentsia, a very contemporary work. From my own experience in Poland, the most contemporary Shakespearean plays have been RICHARD II and RICHARD III — because they deal with what I've called The Great Mechanism, terror, dictatorship, etc. and one tended to identify events in the play with Stalin's purges, the great massacres, despots who claw their way to the top and then quickly topple into the abyss.

Is there a Shakespearean work today that is, as it were, becoming contemporary because of its affinities with current events?

In the past decade, there are at least two Shakespearean plays that have sort of made new careers for themselves. One was TITUS ANDRONICUS and the other, even moreso, TIMON OF ATHENS — plays which, rarely performed before, have taken on a new kind of relevance for modern audiences. THE WINTER'S TALE must also be included; a play even less frequently performed which has, in the past ten years or so, begun to carry a new message and a new fascination; probably because of a new temporal attitude which has developed in regard to Shakespeare. There is some obscurity or darkness in this play, which has now become dazzling and tempting. This is also true of THE TEMPEST, but for different reasons.

And what are those?

One has to do with technological advances in the theatre itself. If one approaches this play traditionally seeing Prospero as a kind of old magus or enchanted Santa Claus-figure, it's of course ridiculous. If we try to make this island merely a kind of enchanted Disneyland, it's just childish. But with the new technology, with lasers and video and other 'special effects', THE TEMPEST becomes ripe for a whole range of new theatrical possibilities. But there is also a new thematic incentive in regard to this play which lends itself to a different ideological interpretation; a new definition of magic, of art, of the power of art, the secrecy of art, the obscurity of art, the creation and re-creation of art, of Theatre as art and symbolically, of Creation itself.

Is it possible for Shakespeare's works to be constantly reinterpreted or does there come a saturation-point; a point at which one simply has to return to the traditional understanding of these plays?

I don't believe in the idea of some staple tradition in Shakespeare, either theatrical or interpretive, which cannot be changed or challenged. First of all, the Shakespearean tradition does not exist. It was lost because of the rupture brought about by the closing of the theatres during Cromwell's time.

Does that mean then there's no such thing as a traditional rendering of a Shakespearean play?

If one believed there could be some kind of traditional interpretation of Shakespeare, it would have to be in English but now we have a theatre of the planet — with festivals and revivals in every conceivable part of the world. Shakespeare exists now in Africa, in India, in Japan — almost any country you care to name.

Do you mean that because Shakespeare has become multi-nationalized — mixed up with so many different cultures and theatrical styles — that it is impossible any longer to conceive of a traditional approach?

Yes.

But isn't it possible through translation to essay a traditional view of Shakespeare's plays? That's to say, a rendition of what we take to be the historically based, received- perception of those works?

No, I don't believe so, and the reason is similar to that which applies to ancient Greek tragedy. We no longer have the tools that were available to a theatre such as the Globe, the wooden 'O', the sexual disguise of boys playing woman's parts etc. Just as we no longer have the amphitheatres which created, and to a certain extent conditioned, the Greek drama. We now have a new medium. The old medium, if merely repeated, creates only museum art.

So by freeing these plays from their original conventions, we have, in a sense, made them universal, is that what you mean?

Yes, I mean just that.

Is it necessary for directors mounting Shakespeare to take account of the plays' historicity? Or is it possible for a director to proceed with no regard whatsoever for the given historical and political background of the works?

There are no rules. It's really a free-for-all. It has a lot to do with the number of Shakespearean productions. If you have only one production of HAMLET a year then, for the sake of the schools, the colleges, the new audience, it has to be what you might call a 'regular' HAMLET. But when you have twenty in a year, even if it were possible to produce a 'traditional' HAMLET, there would be no point in producing twenty identical HAMLETS.

But I mean something else. Let's say a director is preparing a production of HAMLET; *is it really possible for him to ignore the Elizabethan attitudes towards kingship, towards inheritance, towards honor and chivalry — in short, toward all the fundamental values that pertained at that time, and still do justice to the original work?*

I don't know. It seems to me this is different in regard to different Shakespearean plays. It's not the same in the case of the histories, for instance, or in a play such as MACBETH, where you have a king, a royal family, feudal lords, a tower, the landscape of Scotland; elements which exist in the matter of the play. If you transpose all of this into a Sheikdom, let's say, or into some other highly exotic cultural clime, much of the play will become vague or insubstantial. On the other hand, if you take a play like THE COMEDY OF ERRORS, and obediently respect the historical milieu of the work, it will be impossible or boring or, at the very least, irrelevant. We have to place this play into some kind of new environment.

So there are plays of Shakespeare that are pliant and others in which, one cannot so easily break the closed circuit of the original work?

This is exactly my meaning. In the historical plays, the essence of history should be respected — but the essence of feudal history is not necessarily the sad tales of the Lords Anointed. It is dishonest to perform RICHARD III or RICHARD II or HENRY IV without touching on certain parallels to our contemporary time of political terrors, 'les temps des assassins' etc.,

So even if one tried to present a traditional-historical version of RICHARD III, *contemporary associations in the minds of the audience would still be informing the play. People coming to see* RICHARD III *would still come with the knowledge of Stalin and east Europe and Afghanistan.*

You see, the conscious director has to ask himself: what is the historicity and what, the contemporaneity of the play? In RICHARD III for example, what is contemporary is the terror and the persecution; the experience of fear, danger, torture, the entire mechanism of political repression. But the icons of this terror are, of course, the old kings of England. It would be risky to make the face of RICHARD III identical with the face of Josef Stalin. But it would be blind and childish to say this is merely the remote past of the feudal era. Sometimes the analogy is stronger if the identification is not too obvious. Mnouchkine in her last productions of Shakespeare's histories dressed the English kings and Court as samurai in the costumes of the Kabuki. This oriental masquerade seems to me pretentious. It's not the costumes that are so important or the 'faces' of the Lords Anointed but the mechanism of terror. Its faces are both historical and timeless.

So historicity and contemporaneity must go hand in hand in every legitimate classical revival.

Exactly.

Then tell me this. What is scholarship's role in relation to Shakespearean production? Should the scholar be a kind of hovering dramaturg, as for instance you've been in regard to the National Theatre production of AS YOU LIKE IT *and Peter Brook's* KING LEAR? *What kind of function can he or should he perform?*

Again, there are no rules. The ideal dramaturg would combine the skills of both the director and the scholar. But either such people do not exist or cannot exist, or in any case, are very hard to find.

I'm very aware of a very sharp division between professional theatrical production and scholarship. When I occasionally attend symposia or academic get-togethers, I always feel I'm with people from a different solar system than myself. Does such a division have to exist?

There are a few outstanding exceptions to the rule. Granville Barker, for instance who wrote intelligently and even academically on the subject of Shakespeare and was, by all accounts, an excellent director. There's also John Russell Brown who is an excellent scholar and also a professional director. Then there's Georgio Strehler, whose knowledge of the Italian and Renaissance theatre is utterly limitless, and is also one of the great theatre-directors. But I take your point; it's hard to come up with too many examples. It's rather hard to find someone who is a virgin and also very good in bed.

This role of the 'dramaturg' is a very imprecise one. More and more, people feel there should be such a creature attached to a serious theatre, but no one is too sure of precisely how he should function there. How do you see his role?

Again, there are no rules. A dramaturg is a German invention — which probably began in the 19th century when Goethe was appointed to the Court Theatre at Weimar. There are many possible kinds of working-relationships. It's up to the director to hammer out a viable relationship with his dramaturg — one that will work for both of them. But the director, you have to remember, is concerned with acting on stage, bodies in movement. Footnotes exist in a scholastic work; but it's impossible to have them in the theatre. A director can't say: I'm doing it this way but I could just as easily do it this other way. The director has to choose his line and then hoe to it. The director of course, is second only to God — and in some instances, even before Him, so to work out a good relationship with a dramaturg is very difficult. It's more difficult even than marriage — and marriage, as we all know, is difficult enough.

In a lot of recent Shakespearean productions, there has been a new emphasis on decor. It's almost as if stage setting, in the 19th century sense, has returned to our stages. Does this have some kind of special implication?

Two or three years ago, during a Shakespeare Festival at Stratford, Ontario, I saw an extremely elaborate production of MIDSUMMER NIGHT'S DREAM — very rich settings — in many ways reminiscent of Max Reinhardt's production of the thirties. With the rotation of taste, after years of naked sets and Spartan decor, the effect of this sumptuous and elaborate setting was to give us something new and interesting. That's the first point. The second is: in the last decade, there has been an enormous advance in opera — I mean opera as spectacle. When I was young, opera seemed very old-fashioned, very 19th century, something that you went to hear rather than to see. Today it's become highly advanced, extremely elaborate and dominantly visual. Whereas before, the opera was in many ways aping the theatre, now the theatre seems to be aping opera. And of course, many theatre-directors such as Zefferelli, Peter Hall, and Peter Brook to a certain extent move easily from one to the other. In my lifetime, that's to say since about the end of World War II, there was an ideological and philosophical emphasis on contemporary interpretation in Shakespeare; an emphasis on thematic content, on what these plays mean and should mean to modern audiences. And now, because of a certain distrust or disenchantment with ideology, a certain boredom with politics, there is this return to a Shakespeare which is apolitical, non-philosophic, non-ideological. And since, the plays no longer have 'new meanings'; they must at least have new costumes, new settings, new visual expression.

So you believe this new emphasis on decor is compensation for lack of thematic substance?

By and large, I would say so. If not a new message, than at least there should be some new tricks. Remember in THE TEMPEST when Ariel says to Prospero: "What would my potent master? Here I Am." and Prospero replies: "Thou and thy meaner fellows your last service/ did worthily perform, and I must use you/In such another trick. Go bring the rabble..."

But is it a general rule that when you have an extremely elaborate setting, it is concealing a paucity of real content? Aren't there certain kinds of interpretations that demand more elaborate settings — merely to fulfill certain ambitious visual intentions?

Probably you are right — but there's another point here. It's not only that this tendency indicates the end of ideological interpretation, it also marks, in some way, the end of the old avant-garde; by that I mean the avant-garde of the fifties and the sixties. The proponents of this avant-garde were, more or less, restricted to small theatres; the limited resources of the small stage; they weren't involved with large spectacles. Now with the termination of this avant-garde, we are seeing a return to the big spectacle; Robert Wilson, being perhaps the most obvious example of the new avant-garde; an artist whose work demands an extremely expensive, extremely spectacular theatrical form.

It is certainly the impression today that someone like Robert Wilson is the most conspicuous exponent of the 'new' avant-garde, but is his work, strictly speaking, avant-garde? Is it not an amalgam of influences derived

from the sixties and seventies and even earlier? Does his work represent a genuine move in another direction or is it merely a grandiloquent recapitulation of the 'happenings' and multi-media experiments of twenty and twenty-five years ago?

No comment.

I'd like, despite your reticence, to push this subject a little further. I agree with you that today there is nothing quite so clapped-out as the 'avant-garde' work of the sixties. My question is: can any avant-garde replenish itself quite so quickly? Don't a certain number of generations have to go by, assimilating the new innovations, before the next wave of the avant-garde can appear? Is it actually possible for each generation, every ten years or so, to produce its own avant-garde?

It's very hard to answer this because the avant-garde is not simply a new batch of tricks thrown up by the new generation, but a challenge thrown down to the morality, the philosophy, the manners, and the status quo. It is difficult to imagine an avant-garde without a challenge to established values or indeed, to the Establishment itself.

Do you see this happening today?

I personally do not see it.

Would you agree then that, in a sense, the old avant-garde of the fifties and sixties has not, in fact, produced any discernible successors?

I can only say that, speaking for myself, I cannot see any significant avant-garde movement in the original sense of that overused term. But I must admit that for the past five or six years, I have been very cut off from the main stream.

Is this perhaps because it is no longer possible to challenge established values, to 'epater le bourgeois' as used to be done in the last fifty to a hundred years?

But who is the 'bourgeois' today? It is the avant garde itself.

Is it conceivable that the kinds of insurrections we associate with the old avant-garde, which were so culturally disturbing and artistically revolutionary, are no longer possible in a day and age where society is inured to all such shocks?

Probably yes, because as we have all seen in the past decade or so, the bourgeois-marketplace is all powerful; it consumes the avant garde, as it consumes everything else. There is no innovation, no new invention that isn't, in a matter of weeks, packaged, merchandised and distributed to the main stream society.

Is it then the genius of that highly-commercialized society to be able to gobble up avant-garde initiative so rapidly that no challenge to established values can threaten it for very long?

I guess so. There was an article in The New York Times several months ago about some marvelous new painting which was considered a remarkable specimen of avant-garde work, and it was immediately on sale the very next week. What can one say about that when one considers the fate of early avant-garde paintings that had to wait decades for sale, and almost a hundred years for recognition.

I want to return to the subject of Shakespeare. I know that Brooks' KING LEAR *was very much influenced by your book* SHAKESPEARE, OUR CONTEMPORARY, *as was Georgio Strehler's TEMPEST and the National Theatre's production of* AS YOU LIKE IT. *Isn't there something suspect and a bit second-hand about a director basing a production on another man's ideas? Doesn't this in some vague way smack of plagiarism?*

No, not to my mind. Because as we all know, a theatrical production, from no matter how innovative a director, looks for its nourishment wherever it can find it — in current events, in politics, in personal experience, theatrical experience, and so on. Peter Brook who is a genius of eclecticism is perhaps the best example of this.

So you think that taking ideas from a work-of-scholarship is just part and parcel of the overall plagiarism a director indulges in when he assembles a production in the first place?

Yes, because the very essence of the director's work is plagiarism. He plagiarizes the text; he plagiarizes the theatrical tradition; he plagiarizes the experience of his actors. He almost cannot make a move without plagiarizing something or somebody. A theatrical production is, almost by definition, a second-hand work-of-art.

Would you therefore deduce from that, that a director can never be an original creator, but can only be, at best, something of an inspired eclectic?

Some directors create their own theatre. Some of them not only devise mise-en-scene, but create their own physical environment as well, and the theatrical styles that are performed there. So much so that the next generation spends most of it's time plagiarizing their work. Take Meyerhold for example. Many of the directors who came after him were the legitimate or illegitimate children of Meyerhold. Stanislavsky has thousands of legitimate and illegitimate children — especially in this country. Grotowsky has certainly had his plagiarizers. Take Brecht — who to my mind, was the man most responsible for changing the attitudes to Shakespeare in England. It was the Brechtian vision and to a certain extent the Brechtian technology which heavily influenced the staging of Shakespeare all over Europe — from Poland to England.

But what of Brecht's dialectical approach to material — what made him so uniquely Brechtian — do you see that influence as well? Because otherwise, it's only a superficial influence you're referring to.

I don't believe it's all that superficial; not when one is dealing with a new style of acting, a new way of using the stage. The old message and the old vision, — meaning, function and spectacle were challenged. If you try to deal with Shakespearean drama, not through an understanding of the characters but rather through the objective situation which asks us to see the 'unnatural of the natural', as Brecht used to say, that doesn't produce a superficial impact.

Can you cite productions under Brecht's influence, which have reconstituted the material in that way; have made us see it more objectively and from that different perspective?

Yes, in many of the British and Italian productions we often get a Brechtian vision, though never the Brechtian ideology.

To return then to my earlier point: do you think it is legitimate to be Brechtian in appearance and not Brechtian in ideology?

Even during Brecht's own term at the Berliner Ensemble, there were productions which have been true to the Brechtian form but extremely alien to Brecht's ideology. The best example of this is MOTHER COURAGE which never quite achieved the contempt Brecht wanted in regard to his central character.

Are you saying that Brecht himself was never able to produce a truly Brechtian result in his work?

In some ways, yes. The question is still open. But the main heritage of Brecht in the modern theatre is not the political pretensions of Brecht's work, the assault on capitalism etc., but the theatrical matter, the Epic approach that relied heavily on the 'alienation effect' which is perhaps the most important part of the acting legacy.

I want to ask you about certain tendencies in classical interpretations. Can Kurosowa's RAN *really be considered a version of* KING LEAR, *given the fact that it veers away so radically from the original work? At what point does an extrapolation of a Shakespearean work, such as Edward Bond's* LEAR *or Tom Stoppard's* ROSENCRANTZ AND GUILDENSTERN ARE DEAD *or Grotowsky's* DOCTOR FAUSTUS, *become independent works of art with no debt at all to the original?*

Levi-Strauss once said: every interpretation of a myth is a new myth. For example, the Freudian version of the Oedipus and Elektra myths is a new version of those myths. In this larger sense, any ANTIGONE (and we've had about twenty ANTIGONES in modern times) or any ELEKTRA (and there have been several of those in recent years) is a reinterpretation, or rethinking of the original Greek play.

But that is an extrapolation from a myth. What we were talking about is an extrapolation from a given literary work by William Shakespeare.

The only real difference between Shakespeare and the Greek tragedians is that Shakespeare is somewhat closer to us in time. In any case, to my way of thinking, we have to challenge Shakespeare — even if not actually challenging the words themselves. The interpretation should give new meaning without changing the letter of the text. Once I wrote: "We need to rape classics without respect but with love and passion." Now, I would qualify that by saying: we have to force the classical texts to give us new answers. But to obtain new answers, we have to bombard them with new questions. If Shakespeare is translated into Japanese or Hebrew, obviously the director's freedom is greater. If we change the medium from stage to screen, for instance, our freedom is greater still because it is impossible, or just silly merely to transplant a stage-production onto the screen.

To get back to Kurasowa......

To my mind, the greatest, most impressive and illuminating vision of MACBETH is Kurasowa's THRONE OF BLOOD.

And you would still contend that, even though it radically veers away from the original, it is still, in essence, Shakespeare's play?

Kurasowa's film RAN is much further away from the play than Peter Brook's film version of KING LEAR. In some ways, Kurasowa is more faithful to Shakespeare in his movie than Peter Brook is in his. This is also true of Kozintzev's KING LEAR which is, to my mind, one of the greatest screen adaptations of all time.

What pops into my mind is a film of the late forties with, I believe, Paul Douglas, called JOE MACBETH *which was a gangster movie which bore almost no relation to Shakespeare's play but dealt with the rise of a small-time gangster who rubbed out all the other gangsters who stood in his way in order to become top dog. Would you say that a film like that is also a legitimate extrapolation from* MACBETH?

No.

Then what is the dividing-line between an original, independent work and a valid interpretation of a Shakespearean play?

I can answer that best by posing another question: Is WEST SIDE STORY a legitimate interpretation from ROMEO AND JULIET or a completely new work?

The answer for me would be that it's a completely new work.

I don't know what a 'completely new work' is. Shakespeare is always there in the background. One cannot completely obliterate him.

It would appear then, from what you're saying, that one has to examine each one of these 'extrapolations' or 'versions' on its own merits. THE COMEDY OF ERRORS *is not* THE BOYS FROM SYRACUSE, *but this musical has taken Shakespeare's comedy as its springboard just as, I suppose, Shakespeare took Plautus as his springboard. So does one say to Shakespeare: thank you very much for providing us with this story, but we don't really need you any longer as we're going off in another direction. In just the same way as Shakespeare might have said 'thank you' to Belleforest or Kyd or Holinshed or Boccacio.*

Exactly.

Let me ask you this. Do you think that being a Polish critic with a European background gives you a different kind of insight into Shakespeare's work? You have Polish eyes. Does that make you see something different than if you had British or American eyes?

I would suppose at least fifty per cent of what I've written was because of my Polish and European experience. First of all, there's the social and political context of my life. I was in Warsaw with the underground during World War 2 and was constantly involved in politics during the time I lived in Poland. And so naturally, I am a completely different bird compared to the British or American critics. Half of my life-experience has been politics rather than books or spectacles; immersion in real history, not history seen in film or television documentaries.

But can that also mean, given your natural and instinctive political bias, you sometimes see things in Shakespeare's works that are not there?

All partial views are, at the same time, important and incorrect.

And if one wanted to provide a corrective?

It's virtually impossible for a director, and even moreso for a critic, to be 'correct'. If someone wants to be 'correct', they must become a proofreader and not a critic.

Do you mean then there is no such thing as 'correct' ' criticism?

To the best of my knowledge, no such thing exists. Real criticism cannot be, what you would call, correct.

Is there such a thing as fallacious criticism?

If one is not correct, it doesn't follow that one is fallacious. In my mind, not to be 'correct' means a critic may defend, in a more vigorous way than is usually done by so-called impartial critics, the views that he holds. As a critic, you have to be a partisan. In some way, a critic is an advocate or an attorney, but never the presiding judge. He has either to accuse or to defend. No one expects the attorney to be completely fair because his function is either to accuse or to defend. The virtue of fairness is not one of the virtues of the critic.

To take up your own metaphor: there comes a point at the end of a trial when what attorneys have defended or prosecuted becomes the subject of a judgment. Is there some final tribunal for critical ideas where they are ultimately judged to be right or wrong? Correct or incorrect?

This just does not exist.

Prosecution and defense do exist, but judgement does not?

There are no final judgments in criticism.

What, fundamentally, is the use of Shakespeare criticism?

The most obvious answer, which was once formulated by T.B. SPENCER at a Royal Shakespeare conference, is: Shakespeare has three lives. His first life is the theatre. His second life consists of his written works, published and read from one generation to the next, and his third life consists of teaching and criticism. For millions of students all over the world, Shakespeare exists as a text and as a subject for study. It may be sensible or nonsensical, intelligible or unintelligible, but what one cannot deny is that Shakespeare exists, he is a living presence. The average young man who is exposed to Shakespeare during his school or college years, and eventually becomes an old man, keeps some portion of Shakespeare with him to the end of his life.

But what use is he to this young and subsequently old man? Is Shakespeare philosophically important to him? Is his humanism of some value? What is it that's so important about this heritage?

Trivially speaking, Shakespeare is a supermarket. Shakespeare-criticism produces Shakespeare-scholars; Shakespeare-scholars produce Shakespeare-criticism which in turn produces Shakespeare-teachers who go on to become Shakespeare critics and Shakespeare-scholars, and so forth and so on in endless repetition.

It's one of the great multi-national industries.

Of course. Shakespeare was presumably born in Stratford but if someone should prove that he wasn't born in Stratford or that there never was such a person, it would be a disaster — not only culturally but financially as well.

If Shakespeare, it should turn out, were born in Liverpool, let's say, it would be......

An international catastrophe!

You seem to be saying that Shakespeare is like a self-perpetuating and unkillable Frankenstein monster.

In some way, yes. But that is equally true of the universities. As I wrote once, they live by 'eating'. Eating Aristotle, eating Plato, eating Moliere, and eating Shakespeare. It's a gargantuan digestive system.

And they also disgorge at regular intervals.

Without Shakespeare, it would mean the downfall of one-third of the American educational system. He is in many ways the most established figure in the Establishment.

Will Shakespeare always be our contemporary or it conceivable that a time might come when Shakespeare will no longer speak to modern generations? Could Shakespeare become like Seneca or Menander — an archaic old master whose influence might just pass away?

My dear Charles, I will have been many, many years dead before anything like that comes to pass.

HARLOTRY IN BARDOLATRY

or

RECYCLING SHAKESPEARE

Abridged Lecture delivered by Marowitz at the Shakespeare-Tage, Bochum Germany, April 1987

Looking around for a suitable sub-title for this paper I asked a professor of my acquaintance if he could suggest anything and, given the nature of my Shakespearean rewrites, he said: "How about 'Tis Pity He's A Whore?" — I took the liberty of slightly revising that suggestion into the present sub-title.

I don't really think anyone can deny the fact that a good deal of 'harlotry' has insinuated itself into Bardolatry. When you have a large, multi-national corporation such as the Shakespeare Industry, it goes without saying that it attracts people of easy virtue, and that's a subject to which I will shortly return.

As to my credentials, or my lack of them, I have to say that I speak as a professional director — not as a scholar or a pedagogue.

A director's relationship to Shakespearean scholarship (Granville-Barker notwithstanding) is very different from an academic's. For the academic, theories, suppositions, and speculations are ends in themselves, and a really solid piece of Shakespearean criticism need only be well argued and well written to join the voluminous tomes of its predecessors. But a director is looking for what in the theatre are called 'playable values' — that is, ideas capable of being translated into concrete dramatic terms. Very often, scholars provide just that, and there is more 'scholarship' on view in classical productions throughout Europe and America than audiences tend to realize. Most directors prefer to play down the fact that many an original theatrical insight can be traced back, not to a director's leap-of-the-imagination, but to a scholar's dry-as-dust thesis. Three notable and acknowledged lifts immediately spring to mind: Laurence Olivier's Oedipal production of *Hamlet* based on a psychoanalytical tract by Ernest Jones (Hamlet and Oedipus, 1949), Peter Brook's *King Lear*, and The National Theatre's all-male *As You Like It* — both derived in large part from essays in Jan Kott's <u>Shakespeare Our Contemporary</u> (1965)

'Playable values' are not always consistent with literary values. A scholarly insight can make very good sense and be untranslatable in stage-terms. Conversely, a playable value can be brilliantly effective in a mise-en-scene and yet not hold up to intellectual scrutiny afterwards. A classic in production makes demands that are never called for in the study. And perhaps that's where so much of the trouble stems from. And by 'trouble' I mean the traditional animosity that tends to smolder between the professional theatre and the academic community. There is a factor in Shakespearean production which rarely enters into the academic study of a text. It's a stubborn factor and a transforming factor and, unfortunately, one that won't go away. I refer of course to the director.

In the nineteenth century, men such as the Duke of Saxe-Meiningen, Henry Irving, and Herbert Beerbohm Tree were closer to chairmen-of-committees than what we, today, call modern directors. They supervised their actors and decided questions of design but they didn't really insinuate a highly personal viewpoint onto their productions. With the advent of Konstantin Stanislavsky in Russia, Augustin Daly in New York, and Max Reinhardt in Germany, the director, armed with a stylistic prerogative and an aesthetic bias, gradually came to the fore. In the 1920s and 1930s in France, with men such as Jacques Copeau, Charles Dullin, Gaston Baty, Louis Jouvet and Jean-Louis Barrault, and in Russia with Nikolai Evreinov, Eugene Vakhtangov and Vsevolod Meyerhold, we begin to see the first signs of another kind of director: men who leave their mark on material as much as they do on actors; directors who begin to reveal an attitude to new and established plays which is more pronounced than before. Sometimes, aggressively so.

The emergence of what we would call the modern director coincides not with his imposed authority on the physical elements of production, but his intercession with a playwright's ideas. The old autocrat-director controlled his actors; the modern director appropriates to himself those intellectual ingredients usually reserved for the playwright — using the tangible instruments of the stage as a kind of penmanship with which he alters or gives personal connotation to the text of writers both living and dead.

This is most visible in the works of Shakespeare and with directors such as Max Reinhardt, Benno Besson, Giorgio Strehler, Peter Stein, and Peter Brook: men who began to produce resonances in established works which surprised audiences that never imagined the plays dealt with the themes they *now* seemed to be about. So that, for instance, there comes a production of King Lear which charts the rise of the bourgeoisie and the gradual disintegration of feudalism, or another production which treats the play as an Oriental fable entirely detached from any historical milieu, or a version in which it's seen as a bleak, apocalyptic vision unfolding in an arid, Beckettian landscape from which God has been banished.

In these instances, and in many others like them, what has changed is the philosophical framework in which the play was originally conceived; the 'spirit' of the work radically re-routed even though the 'letter' remains intact. In short, another 'author' has appeared, and he is saying things different from — sometimes at conflict with — the meanings of the first author, and this interloper is, of course, the modern director; a man who insists on reading his own thoughts into those traditionally associated with the author whose work he is communicating.

A director who does not proceed in this way, who chains himself to unwavering fidelity to the author and pursues his work in selfless devotion to the 'meaning of the text' is unknowingly abdicating a director's responsibility. Since the only way to express an author's meaning is to filter it through the sensibility of those artists charged with communicating it, 'fidelity' is really a high-sounding word for lack-of-imagination. The director who is committed to putting the play on the stage exactly as it is written is the equivalent of the cook who intends to make the omelet without cracking the eggs. The modern director is the master of the subtext as surely as the author is of the text, and his dominion includes every nuance and allusion transmitted in each moment of the performance. He's not simply a person who imposes order upon artistic subordinates in order to express a writer's meaning, but someone who challenges the assumptions of a work-of-art and uses mise-en-scene actively to pit his beliefs against those of the play. Without that confrontation, that sense of challenge, true direction cannot take place, for unless the author's work is engaged on an intellectual level equal to his own, the play is merely transplanted from one medium to another — a process which contradicts the definition of the word 'perform' — which means to 'carry on to the finish', to 'accomplish' — to fulfill the cycle of creativity begun by the author.

The great Shakespearean pastime has always been tendency-spotting — the intellectual equivalent of bird-watching — and anyone who's been hard at it has discovered the tendency, for example, towards bigger and more elaborate stage-settings; toward politicizing the histories; towards sexualizing the mixed-gender comedies, etc., etc. But the tendency that interests me most is the separation that's begun to take place between the original plays and works on which they are loosely — sometimes remotely — based. To explain this tendency, I think it's useful to look at the recent TV adaptations of the collected works produced by the BBC.

The great lesson of those filmed Shakespearean plays is that, in refusing to allow the material to transform — to adapt itself to a different medium — most of the works were denatured. One could praise this performance or that scenic idea, but all in all, it produced leaden and inert television viewing. And why? Because the underlying assumption of the exercise was: the plays are so great, all one need do is bring together the best British talent one can find and record them for posterity. It is this high-varnish approach to Shakespeare, which is his chiefest foe — the detestable conservative notion that all one ever needs do with 'classics' is preserve them.

One ought to be clear about this: The bastions that protect William Shakespeare have been well and truly established by scholars, critics, teachers, litterateurs — people with a vested interest in language and the furtherance of a literary tradition. It's in their interests that the texts remain sacrosanct — that they are handed down from generation to generation, each providing new insights and new refinements like so many new glosses on an old painting. A process which, judging from the past two hundred years, can go on for at least another five hundred because there will never be a shortage of scholars to point out the semiotic significance of the ass's head in A Midsummer Night's Dream or the tallow candle in Macbeth or the implications of the syllabus at Wittenberg University during the years Hamlet was enrolled there.

In Academe, as I'm sure I needn't tell you, it is considered a step-up-the-ladder to the published in learned journals. It's a help in securing tenure and a fillip towards university advancement.

Consequently, the motive for publication is very much like that of a showcase production for an ambitious actor; a way of strutting his stuff — often at the expense of the material for which that 'stuff' is being 'strutted'. There is very little compulsion behind this kind of Shakespearean scholarship other than scoring points or sticking feathers in one's cap. Often, the writer's underlying aim is merely to catch the attention of a department head or a fund-granting agency. What you might call 'harlotry' in bardolatry'. This accounts for the bizarre nature of many of those precious and far-fetched subjects. Then, of course, there is also that peculiar breed of niggling intellectual which actually enjoys picking at the chicken-bones of art in order to re-create a semblance of the whole bird. This breed accounts for many of those microscopic studies of Shakespearean works that seem to be obsessed with every grain, every wart, every follicle to be found in the collected works. They produce the papers that scrutinize the punctuation, the typography, the syntax and the topical allusions of every play. Not only do they not see the trees for the forests; they're often too fascinated by the sap on the bark to even see the trees. But for people without such obsessions, whose main concern is reconstituting Shakespeare's main ideas and finding new ways to dramatically extrapolate them, this myopic preoccupation with the canon seems, more than anything else, like the scrutiny of one chimpanzee fastidiously picking the nits off another.

But to return to Shakespeare and the media. Had the BBC treated the plays as 'material' to be refashioned for a new medium, had they not felt obligated to freeze them for posterity, each one might have been a unique televisual experience without losing the essence of the stage-work on which it was based. A method more successfully practiced in motion pictures.

If you do a swift comparison of the early Shakespearean films with the later ones, you find that the biggest single difference is that in the 1930s there was a valiant attempt to stick to the narrative and, as much as possible, to the text, and these are virtually unwatchable today. But from about the 1940s onward, filmmakers were more inclined to depart from the original texts and move off into purely cinematic directions. Which is why, for instance,

Olivier's Richard III is so much better than Hollywood's As You Like It with Elisabeth Bergner, directed by her husband Paul Czinner, or Romeo and Juliet, starring a somewhat superannuated Norma Shearer and Leslie Howard. In Richard III, Olivier truncated the text, decided on three or four main character-points, and then expanded the battle scenes with a kind of inspired, epic film-making: the same scenes which on the stage usually consist of perfunctorily choreographed duels which almost always stop dead the action of the play. What Shakespearean filmmakers discovered was that the more one expanded the cinematic possibilities and the less one felt restricted by the straitjacket of the text, the better the work was realized.

What is it for instance, about Kurosawa's Ran, that Japanese director's treatment of King Lear, which makes it a reinterpretation of Shakespeare's play and, at the same time, a bold diversion into a completely new work of art? For me, it's the liberty that Kurosawa exercises in following the play wherever, in his own personal imagination, it takes him. And if the imagination of an artist is rich and resourceful, it leads him to a highly personalized statement on the play's themes that could never have been made without taking the play as its point of departure.

Writing about this film, Jan Kott says:

Kurosawa's greatness lies in his capacity to reveal a historical similarity and variance; to find a Shakespearean sense of doom in the other, remote, and apparently alien historical place. He trims the plot to the bone. Hidetora's three sons are all that remains of Lear's three daughters and Gloucester's two sons. Shakespeare added the second plot of Gloucester, Edgar, and Edmund to the old folk tale about three daughters (two vile and one noble). Kurosawa has cut and compressed it. In this Japanese condensation of plot and character, only the eldest wife's son, a substitute for Goneril and Regan, is left in the castle where Hidetora has murdered her entire family. In this samurai epic, it is her drive for vengeance that destroys Hideotora's clan and legacy. (Jan Kott, 'The Edo Lear', New York Review of Books (24 April 1986), pp. 13-15.)

And, discussing the distancing of Shakespeare's play by radically altering its setting, Kott says:

"In Shakespeare's dramas, the other place — the other 'historicity' outside Elizabethan England — gives, at the same time, the plays' other universality. And what is more, the place often supplies their other contemporary meanings...The farther the 'other' setting in Shakespeare's dramas is from Elizabethan England, the less likely it is that the image will match the text. It stops being an illustration and becomes its essence and sign.

Its 'essence' and "sign'! The whole assumption of these words is that it's possible to retain a play's essence by changing its 'sign'. Indeed, it is by changing its sign that its essence is both retained and enlarged. It is through a classic's imaginative metamorphosis that its eternal verities shine through. And, I would say, the reverse proposition is also true; that by trying to contain those verities in their original enclosure they become attenuated and reduced. Because as one generation supplants another, as new ideas force us to test the validity, or at least durability, of the old ones, artists are obliged to verify or nullify what they find in the old works. This 'verification' or 'nullification' is what determines the nature of the new work — and, in an inexplicable way, it often reinforces the integrity of the original.

The advantage that films have over plays is that the medium insists the original material be rethought and then expressed differently. The disadvantage in the theatre is that there's a kind of premium put on some abstract notion called 'fidelity' — which from the standpoint of the purists seems again to mean: make the omelet but don't break the eggs. The only fidelity that cuts any ice in the theatre is a director's fidelity to his personal perceptions about a classic; how well and how truly he can put on stage the visions the play has evoked in his imagination. How much of those visions have to do with him and how much with Shakespeare remains an inexhaustible moot point, and there's nothing to be gained from delving into that one now. The central point, it seems to me, and the one that determines the validity or nullity in the final result is: what added dimensions does the director bring to the original work? If, as is so often the case, a director's imagination falls short of the work he's trying to realize, then he deserves all the calumny that is gleefully heaped upon his head. If he manages to transcend it — and makes something of it that was never expected and never seen before — he has enriched a classic. And if the word classic has any meaning at all it must refer to a work that is able to <u>mean again,</u> and perhaps mean something else.

To combat such subversive ideas we have the counter-argument succinctly put by Maynard Mack. He writes:

"*The most obvious result of subtextualizing is that the director and (possibly) actor are encouraged to assume the same level of authority as the author. The sound notion that there is a life to which the words give life can with very little stretching be made to mean that the words the author set down are themselves simply a search for the true play, which the director must intuit in, through, and under them. Once he has done so, the words become to a degree expendable.... In the hands of many directors in today's theatre, where the director is a small god, subtext easily becomes a substitute for text and a license for total directorial subjectivity.*"

(Maynard Mack, King Lear In Our Time (Berkeley,1965; London, 1966)

For Maynard Mack and others of his ilk, the play is a 'given' and as such, there is a tacit obligation to deliver its original intentions. For contemporary directors, it's an invitation to undergo process, and only when <u>that</u> is done can its 'meaning' be understood, and because theatrical process is inextricable from contemporary sensibility, the play is either proven or disproven through the act of interpretation. When Antonin Artaud exclaimed: 'No more masterpieces', he not only meant we must lose our myopic reverence for classics, he also meant the Present, like a Court of Appeal, must confirm or deny the presumed greatness of a 'masterwork.' The hard evidence for such an appeal is the director's view of the work as performed by his company and received by his public. Often in such cases, it is the interpreter's vision that is rejected and the masterwork, in all its traditional greatness, which is confirmed. But just as often, it is the artist's metamorphosis of the masterwork that wins the day and when that happens, the director and his actors do, in Maynard Mack's words, "assume the same level of authority as the author." To view this as some kind of usurpation of proprietary rights is to misunderstand the nature of dramatic art and its tendency endlessly to reappear in different shapes and forms.

There are basically two assumptions about Shakespearean production. The first, what one might call the Fundamentalist View, is that if a director cleaves to what the author has written, delves deeper into the complexities of the text and discovers more nuance and more shades of meaning than his predecessors, he has rendered a service to the author and reestablished the supremacy of the work. (Many of the Royal Shakespeare Company productions fall into this category.) The second, what one might call the Reform Approach, assumes that an ingenious director, by interpolating ideas of his own often far removed from the ideas traditionally associated with the play, can sometimes produce a *frisson* — or 'alienating effect' — which is so enthralling in itself, people are prepared to forgive the liberties he's taken to achieve it. Set against these two, now fairly standard, practices is what I would call The Quantum Leap Approach to Shakespeare by which an idea, inspired by the text, but not necessarily verifiable in relation to it, creates a work of art that intellectually relocates the original play and bears only the faintest resemblance to its progenitor. There have been a few examples of this kind of work but each so unlike the other that no general definition can as yet be formulated.

Edward Bond's Lear is an entirely original work, and yet it still feeds off certain ideas of class and cruelty served up in Shakespeare's original play. Tom Stoppard's Rosencrantz and Guildenstern Are Dead, despite its autonomy as a work of art, remains thematically related to Hamlet and still operates within the orbit of the original work where, for instance W.S. Gilbert's Rosencrantz and Guildenstern, being an out-and-out parody, does not. You could say of Brecht's Edward II or Coriolanus that they are intensifications of certain aspects of the works on which they are based — but they still derive most of their power from the reference point of the original. Whereas, in a work like The Resistible Rise of Arturo Ui, although Richard III is knocking around somewhere in the background, the play's historical vigor owes more to the author's assembly of contemporary political history than it does to The Wars of the Roses.

But much closer to the kind of transmutations I'm talking about are works such as Kiss Me Kate — which can be seen as a brilliant riff on The Taming Of The Shrew, and West Side Story which uses only very general elements from Romeo and Juliet (social unrest, family-feuds, etc.) to confront contemporary issues of juvenile delinquency, gang warfare, and ethnic clashes. In a film such as Forbidden Planet, a science-fiction movie of the 1950s, one has all the narrative threads and many of the relationships from The Tempest without actually treading on any of Shakespeare's turf. Knowledge of the ur-text here may enhance a filmgoer's appreciation but it's just as keen for people who never heard of the original. But all these examples are a little off the mark, for as soon as you have an entirely new wodge of material, a completely different format — that is, a musical form as opposed to straight drama, a movie rather than a theatre piece — you're really in the world of allusion and that practice, given the habits of the Greek and Roman dramatists, is as old as drama itself.

Let us take a play like The Tempest for instance: If you consider it from a contemporary standpoint, it's hard not to be struck with what we today would call its psychological symbolism. Connotations of the Ego and the Id have been read into this play for quite some time now. Now, what might the fable of that play be if we remorselessly rethink it along those lines?

In a kind of private sanitarium stuck away in a rustic setting such as Surrey or Hampshire, we encounter a man who suffers from a curious delusion — not unlike Pirandello's Henry IV. He imagines himself shipwrecked on a desert island of which he has become the absolute ruler. Prospero's 'condition' has been brought about by the trauma of having lost his power to his scheming brother Antonio. To avoid the social consequences of that loss and to help him psychologically assimilate it, he creates a fantasy-world, and he peoples it with characters that relate to his condition. There is a good and blameless daughter with whom he strongly identifies. She, like himself, is an innocent, the antithesis of the scheming, usurping and villainous brother who, unlike Miranda, knows all the ways of the world and how to turn them to his own advantage. There is an attendant 'spirit' that will do his bidding for him; exercise the power that he has lost. There is a personification of his own basest nature; that part of him which he recognizes as being full of vindictiveness against his wrongdoers and is, at the same time, the deeply suppressed alter-ego of his enlightened and intellectual self. (Which not only accounts for Caliban, but explains why he threatens Miranda, that thinly disguised symbol of Prospero's own virtue.) And in this fantasy-world, peopled by psychic extensions of his own enemies and ideals, he creates a situation in which he can take revenge against those that have wronged him; can, as all psychotics do in day-dreams, 'right the wrongs of the real world' through imaginary actions in his fantasy realm.

However, amidst all this delusion, Prospero is forced to confront his own inadequacies; that in his former position conveniently projected into the guise of the Duke of Milan, he was very ill suited to his job — being more concerned with books and intellectual pursuits than the humdrum business of politics; that, in a sense, being usurped by his brother was not entirely attributable to Antonio's villainy but could, in some way, be traced back to his own lack of qualifications. (Which is perhaps why he lays such arduous chores on Ferdinand who is trying to prove himself to the virtuous Miranda — that fantasy projection of Prospero himself.) And when his delirium has run its full course and he has liberated himself from the irresponsible freedoms he preferred to the duties of his former position and confronted the frustrations and aggressions of his own base nature — that is, freed his Ariel and rehabilitated his Caliban — he is ready to return to the real world; the world in which he must abandon his fantasies and assume his responsibilities. This is why he asks for his 'hat' — that traditional symbol of social respectability, and his 'sword,' the practical weapon of defense which, from that point on, will serve him instead of his magical staff. The end of The Tempest, like the end of any psychotic delirium, restores the patient to the known world with a greater measure of self-awareness than when he left it.

Now this remorselessly Freudian reading of Shakespeare's play, I would suggest to you, can be played out in a single, contemporary room, in modern dress, with Prospero on a couch and a silent psychiatrist alongside, without any magical or spectacular accouterments, with a few bits of furniture and some salient bits of modern attire to dramatize our protagonist's voyage from fantasy to reality. As a reading of the play, it's as valid as setting the play on another planet with all the characters in spacesuits (as has been done in several American university productions), or setting it on a Caribbean island full of characters drawn from a turn-of-the-century naval battalion with Caliban as an insubordinate military lout and Ariel as Prospero's dutiful cabin-boy. (Jonathan Miller.) For in all these far-fetched extrapolations of Shakespeare's play, there is some unmistakable line, which, stretched as it may be to breaking-point, still connects up to the themes and ideas contained in the original material. The validity or nullity of these far-ranging interpretations depends on the consistency of a director's mise-en-scene: how much of a piece he can make of that vision which he sees staring back at him when he gazes into the ruffled pool of Shakespeare's play, *The Tempest.*

Let's take another example: *A Midsummer Night's Dream* which itself has gone through quite a few permutations — and was recently transmogrified by Woody Allen in the film: *A Midsummer Night's Sex Comedy* — and if Woody Allen can reinterpret Shakespeare, one wonders with trepidation, can Mel Brooks far behind? We've had dark *Dreams* that emphasized the labyrinth of the forest, and bright *Dreams,* like Peter Brook's magically-Meyerholdian version of 1970, and inevitably, throwbacks to rustic *Dreams* where the nineteenth century version of the play were reasserted with a vengeance. But let's say, drawing on the sexual mysteries contained in the work, one chose to interpret it in a decidedly pre-Christian — even decadent — manner, insinuating rather than uncovering ideas. According to this reading, the story of the play might run something like this:

Oberon, a vindictive homosexual chieftain who exerts immense authority among his circle of followers in the forest, has tried repeatedly to wrest a beautiful Indian boy from his former lover, now rival, Titania — who is himself a homosexual given to dressing up in women's clothes. Titania's refusal to give up the youth or share him with others (the previously established sexual convention) has incensed Oberon and caused irremediable friction between both camps.

To wreak the revenge burning in his bosom, Oberon arranges through Puck (not an ethereal sprite at all, but a superannuated and embittered slave) to administer a potent aphrodisiac to Titania which causes him to become sexually obsessed with the first creature he encounters. Because of his dotage and incompetence (as well as the imprecise nature of Oberon's instructions), Puck administers the drug to two of the four refugees who have wandered into the wood to escape the arbitrary measures being meted out by the State. This causes a series of promiscuous imbroglios; presumably uncharacteristic of the four persons involved

Eventually, through guile, Oberon manages to appropriate the boy for himself, and Titania, now caught in the spell of the aphrodisiac, becomes enamored of an amateur actor, one of several rehearsing a play in the forest, who has been transformed into a beast by the vindictive Puck. Having now acquired the coveted youth who is the unquestionable cause of all the play's strife, Oberon takes pity on Titania's condition, releases (him) from the spell, and the old, sharing homosexual relationship is restored. The wood, transformed into an erotic labyrinth which seems inevitable given the proclivities of Oberon and Titania, encourages the lovers to pursue their carnal and licentious desires until Puck lifts their spell. Once returned to Athens, freed from the diabolical influence of the wood and no longer forced into arbitrary bonding, the lovers settle back to enjoy the entertainment laid on for the Duke's wedding, but Puck, in a final act of vindictiveness, upsets the performance of the play, terrorizes the wedding guests and reminds them that despite their heterosexual celebrations, nefarious, anti-social spirits such as himself are the true rulers of the world and characters such as Theseus and Hippolyta only its figureheads.

A preposterous imposition, I can hear some of my listeners muttering to themselves; a travesty of a play that deals with visions of Arcadia and rustic innocence. And yet, as many scholars agree, the <u>Dream</u> is a play about forbidden fruits — (no pun intended), about promiscuity, bestiality, the slaking of carnal appetites, all those irrepressible desires that society firmly represses in order to ensure an orderly perpetuation. Midsummer Night, as the

Scandinavians know better than most, is a night of unmitigated revelry in which the most potent sexual and anti-social cravings are released. Shakespeare, being a bourgeois writing for a bourgeois public, had to cloak the expression of these pernicious desires within a framework of 'a dream' to make them acceptable, but it's a thin disguise and the whiff of amorality fairly wafts through the musk and the foliage. And what is love-in-idleness if not an aphrodisiac? 'Idleness' means going nowhere, unproductive, unfruitful — sex for fun and not for procreation. Puck, a character derived from an ancient medieval devil, is the incarnation of our most demonic nature; an old embittered and cruel flunky who delights in creating confusion and moral disarray. Like a superannuated Ariel, he is Oberon's recidivist — a 'lifer' who, unlike Prospero's sprite, can never have his sentence commuted. He talks about putting a girdle around the earth in forty minutes, but this is empty braggadocio; a pathetic throwback to the alacrity and fleetfootedness, he once had but has long since lost.

And of course, the amorality of Oberon and Titania is reflected in the surface society in which smug, privileged, upper-middle-class youths play sexual musical-chairs and of which Theseus and Hippolyta are — respectively — the kingpin and queenpin. When they were themselves — before Puck's nefarious influence was imposed — they 'played at' romance and courtship, blithely circulating from one lover's bed to the other. Demetrius allegedly 'made love' to Helena before becoming besotted with Hermia, and Lysander effortlessly switches to Helena under the influence of a mesmerizing aphrodisiac but, as we know, persons under hypnosis can only perform acts basically consistent with their character. The lure of the wood and the spell of the drug merely release the lust and lechery that were always latent.

Even in the case of the Establishment figures, the scent of amorality is overpowering. Before the present distribution of sexual partners, we are told that Oberon is supposed to have lusted after Hippolyta even as Titania did after Theseus.

The tumult in the world — vividly expressed in Titania's speech 'These are the forgeries of jealousy' etc. — which results from Oberon's feud with Titania, represents the conflict of the ordered universe confounded by the Spirit of Anarchy and its concomitant is untrammeled sexuality. There is an even deeper reverberation; the opposition between heterosexual love and homosexual license. Oberon, Titania, and their followers represent the homosexual oligarchy which flourished before heterosexuality became the dominant sexual fashion. The phantoms of that older order still cling to the underside of life and though active only under cover of darkness, they manage to exert their influence and project treacheries against the new social order. The carnality, the bestiality, the rustic romps through morally deregulated terrains, the vague sense of orgy and riot which issue from the now forbidden love of man for man constantly subverts the rosy colored image of heterosexual harmony which was the cover story, not only of Elizabethan theatre but Elizabethan life as well. The Dream, like all dreams, is a repression of unacceptable sexual behavior which, since it could never be stamped out, had to be heavily disguised and, as it were, propagandized out of existence — and Shakespeare's harmonic Christian monogamy was an obvious form of camouflage.

To many, this fanciful view of the sexual polarities of A Midsummer Night's Dream will seem entirely absurd. And yet every time I read the play, I kept coming back to this beautiful Indian boy and Oberon's fanatical desire to have him. I would propose to you that, fanciful as it may seem, such a scenario can be played out within the textual framework of Shakespeare's play — with virtually nothing to contradict it. (As it was, in fact, at the Odense Theatre in Denmark in 1985.) And that seems to me to be one of the acid tests of interpretation. If the play cooperates in its own seduction, both director and material are permitted to have their fling. If the play resists, puts up insuperable obstacles and simply refuses to play along, obviously, the honorable course is to desist. Although, without meaning to give offense, I should add that on certain occasions, I have known classics to be seduced to their everlasting benefit. A few seasons ago The Karamazov Brothers, a traveling juggling-and-vaudeville company, worked over The Comedy Of Errors to everyone's delectation — and some seasons back in New York, a streetwise version of Two Gentlemen Of Verona full of ethnic vernacular and topical jokes, received some discourteous treatment which didn't altogether go amiss. But whether convoluted within the original work or compounded into an entirely different work, the tendency, as I perceive it, is to scatter Shakespearean seeds into new soil and see what amazing new horticulture will sprout.

It is a notion that the diehards will resist with their last breath, but what seems clear to me is: what is essential in the better works of William Shakespeare is a kind of imagery-cum-mythology which has separated itself from the written word and can be dealt with by artists in isolation from the plays that gave it birth. And, by insisting on the preservation of the Shakespearean language, as if the greatness of the plays were memorialized only there, the theatre is denying itself a whole slew of new experiences and new artifacts which can be spawned from the original sources, in exactly the same way that Shakespeare spawned his works from Holinshed, Boccaccio, Kyd, and Belleforest; the future of Shakespearean production lies in abandoning the written works of William Shakespeare and devising new works which are tangential to them, and the stronger and more obsessive the Shakespeare Establishment becomes, the more it will hold back the flow of new dramatic possibilities which transcend what we call, with a deplorable anal-retentiveness, the canon.

WHAT COLOR IS OTHELLO?

Conversation between Kott and Marowitz

The received wisdom about OTHELLO *is that its theme is jealousy. There is Othello's jealousy towards Desdemona, Bianca's towards Cassio, Iago's towards Emilia, Cassio and, some would contend Desdemona as well. But it could just as easily be seen as a play about good and evil, cynicism and gullibility, status and personal image. What do you think it's about?*

There's one point on which most critics generally agree and that is that there is some kind of discrepancy at the root of this play. To paraphrase Bradley: many feel though it is great theatre, it isn't quite great tragedy. One's first impression is that everything appears quite simple but when we look a little a little deeper, everything is thrown into doubt. A good starting-point for trying to sort out this confusion is the character of Othello himself.

We get a great deal of information about him from Iago, from Brabantio, from the Duke. And from Othello himself. What is the great mystery?

I guess the first mystery is his color which is a problem both for audiences and for directors. When you read the play, the question of color may not seem to be a major stumbling-block, but when you come to stage this play, the question of color becomes a very specific decision which the director and actor have to make, and it affects larger issues like the style of acting to be adopted.

Shakespeare tells us in his title that he is a Moor — isn't this sufficient?

Taken in light of the criticism that has accumulated over three hundred years, it clearly is not sufficient. What, after all, is a Moor? And particularly a Moor in Venice for, as you knows, for many years and particularly in the Restoration period, the play was known as 'The Moor of Venice'. Does 'Moor of Venice' have certain parallels with Shakespeare's other nominations such as the 'Prince of Denmark,' the 'Merchant of Venice,' and so forth?

In England at the time of the play's creation, many of the Moors in England were of Spanish origin — Spanish exiles — or some form of Arab. In Shakespeare's time in England, Moors were usually taken to be blackamoors — which may well have been a very different kind of Moor altogether. Now the shift from an Arab of royal blood to an African Moor or a Spanish exile is very considerable. What I am saying is that until you decide on what kind of black man this is, you cannot really decide precisely how you are going to play him.

Two obvious possibilities immediately present themselves — either you can see him as a Moor from Venice — that's to say a foreigner, a stranger, a person different from the main stream society, or a *contodora* — a general hired to fight a particular enemy — like a mercenary.

Olivier cut through all those academic distinctions and simply said: I am going to present this man as a contemporary black. Isn't it permissible simply to roll the Moor, the Arab the Spaniard into a contemporary black?

It is impossible to understand Othello without recognizing his foreignness or strangeness. He makes mention of it in that early scene with Brabantio when he says:

> "....I spoke of most disastrous chances,'
>
> Of moving accidents by blood and field
>
> Of hairbreadth scapes i' th'imminent deadly breach
>
> Of being taken by the insolent foe
>
> And sold to slavery, of my redemption thence
>
> And portance in my travel's history
>
> Wherein of anters vast and deserts idle,
>
> Rough quarries, rocks, and hills whose heads touch heaven,
>
> It was my hint to speak. Such was my process.
>
> And of the Cannibals that each other eat,
>
> The Anthropophagi, and men whose heads
>
> Grew beneath their shoulders."

And in his final monologue, he refers to it again. He is not a natural member of the society in which he functions, and this is important.

However he's extremely useful to that society. Without him, The Duke doesn't seem to be able to conduct his wars. Even though not 'of' the society, he appears to be completely integrated with it and necessary to its military maneuvers. Doesn't that make him less of an outsider?

You could say that he is necessary to that society but he is not actually *integrated* into that society nor wholly accepted by it. This is clearly established in that first dialogue between Iago and Brabantio when he talks about "an old black ram…tupping a white ewe"...and Brabantio's daughter being "covered with a Barbary horse" and being "neighed at" by his nephews. He is necessary to that society because of his prowess and his military skills, but he is not really part of that society. He is not a Venetian. He's in that deliciously ambiguous state of being both *in* the society and *outside* of it at the same time — which is a little like the Jews' situation in Europe before the creation of Israel.

It strikes me that, throughout this play, black is white and white is black. Although abused for his blackness, Othello is essentially good — in the sense that 'white' is symbolically characterized as virtuous, open and good. Iago is white on the outside, but black on the inside. In suggesting that we have to try to distinguish between appearances and reality, was Shakespeare deliberately using color in a metaphorical way?

But I don't accept that distinction between black and white — the black skin and the white soul and vice verse etc.

But in Shakespeare's time, metaphorically speaking, wouldn't you accept that black, suggested treachery, evil, darkness, night; and white, radiance, daylight, openness?

I don't believe that morality can be simplified in that way — even in Shakespeare's time. What does seem clear is that Othello's soul, especially from the middle of the play onward, is savage. The real opposition here is between the noble moor and the rude savage.

And the psychological movement of the play, particularly when Iago has begun to peak Othello's jealousy, is between his primitive instincts and his civilized nature. One moment he has sublime and lyrical poetry, and the next he is venting a maniacal urge for destruction.

Shakespeare is constantly reminding us of the more primitive roots that lie beneath the cultivated general. Jealousy was a common ingredient in Elizabethan drama and can be found in many characters in many plays so there's nothing particularly distinctive about that — but in Othello, it is expressed in an extremely violent form of behavior.

In early 19th century productions of the play in France, Othello murdered Desdemona with a dagger because for the civilized French of that period, strangulation was too intolerable. Now, as far as I know, there is no other play in which a wife or unfaithful mistress is killed in so rude a way as in 'Othello'. If Othello didn't possess this barbaric nature, there would be other, less violent ways of disposing of Desdemona but in the final scenes of the play, Shakespeare strongly emphasizes his primitive nature.

But there are compensations for that savagery. He is extremely chivalrous with Desdemona when they both arrive in Cyprus — extremely civil to Brabantio — elegant and civilized in his appearances before The Duke and the Senate. When we see him behaving in a primitive way, it is because he has been goaded to it by Iago.

A primitive person or a man with a barbaric nature is civilized only until a certain breaking point is reached. Many critics have asked in the past: what is the true nature of Othello? — Is it the civilized facade or the barbaric and savage inner man? The answer of course, is both.

Is Lear not primitive and savage when he hurls down curses on the heads of his daughters? In those moments, he is just as extreme as Othello — calling on the gods to inflict barrenness or spawn demons that will torment their mother. Isn't that primitive behavior?

King Lear also has this double time status. Because on the one hand, he is a Celtic king, before civilization has completely evolved and on the other hand, as is often the case in Shakespeare, this is a Victorian play unfolding in a Victorian court.

In the l7th century?

As I've said before, in Shakespeare we're always dealing with double time. In one sense, it is Venice, and yet it is really London. In one sense, MIDSUMMER NIGHT'S DREAM is set in Athens and at the same time, it takes place in Stratford. Contemporary England is always there to some degree — even in plays dealing with ancient subjects such as CORIOLANUS.

Othello's primitive nature is, of course a given. He talks about witchcraft and spells, and there's that whole sequence about the magical handkerchief, etc — -

Precisely, it is there from the start and so it is simply a matter of how much one chooses to emphasize it. To the best of my knowledge, the greatest emphasis on the character's blackness was made by Olivier at The National Theatre. You remember there was that scene towards the end when Othello enters Desdemona's bedroom with a rose in his mouth, undulating his hips, behaving almost like a savage king. All of that seems to me very unnecessary especially if you compare it, for instance, with the pictures we have of the Edmund Kean interpretation where Othello is almost non-black and, from all we can gather, very un-savage — almost like an Englishman, in fact.

Which approach do you think is the more appropriate?

Nothing in Shakespeare can be said to be more or less appropriate. In Shakespeare, you can always go a little too far, not far enough, whatever.

Were there any dramatic advantages to Olivier's emphasis on Othello's blackness? In depicting him as that noble savage?

A lot of things, as you know, are acceptable in one decade that become unacceptable two decades later. If you look at Olivier's film of HENRY V — full of its picture-book pageantry and patriotic fervor — it was completely acceptable at the time it was made — during the war. But if you compare it with Branagh's HENRY V, you see a very different kind of Henry and a very different attitude to the central character. Today, after Korea and Vietnam, we have a much more ambiguous attitude towards patriotism and towards war. We are much less sympathetic towards that kind of emphasis on Othello's blackness than we were five decades ago. We are more inclined now to consider the character's strangeness or alienation from his white society.

And in fact, more inclined to consider Desdemona's viewpoint than her husband's.

Exactly. We tend to be less impressed by the character's heroic stature — the heroism of the Great Warrior. We have become rather suspicious of these kinds of traits today.

Iago, as he himself says "is nothing if not critical' and throughout the play, his organizing intellect is the motor behind events. Despite his villainy, his being a kind of Machiavellian monster, don't you feel Iago's cynicism emerges as a much more powerful force than Othello's vulnerability or Desdemona's goodness?

There I agree completely. Iago is, far and away, the most fascinating character in the play. Now we all know that in Cinthio, Shakespeare's source for the play, Iago was covetous of Desdemona — and this was the primary motivation behind his actions. But for Olivier as well as other directors, Iago is sometimes obsessed with Othello in a way that lends itself to homosexual interpretation. Iago's relation to his wife is cynical, or neutral or leastwise, nonsexual. He is constantly expressing his contempt for women which, for Olivier and others, suggests a kind of half-conscious, unconscious, homosexual tendency. So we are asked to believe that one of the reasons Iago hates Desdemona is that she has stolen Othello's affection away from himself.

Does such an idea really wash?

No, not to my mind, but Olivier was a great actor and a quite good director and this is simply one of the permutations possible in mounting this play. But whatever doubts we may have about that interpretation, we have to acknowledge that for many critics, Iago's lack of motivation is a central fault in the play.

It was Coleridge, wasn't it, who described him as having a "motiveless malignancy". Could it be that the embodiment of evil that one finds in Iago is a throwback to a figure from the Morality Plays where characters personified abstract qualities such as goodness and evil.

It's possible but difficult to prove, however there's a rather significant point in regard to OTHELLO. It is one of the few Shakespearean plays where, alongside the cast-list, you have descriptions of the characters. Iago is defined there as a villain. One view of this could simply be that a villain is a villain because he's a villain — just as a rose is a rose is a rose. Of course, we have the information that he was passed up for the job of lieutenant and so there is a certain amount of professional rancor against Othello on that score. Also he suspects Othello has slept with Emilia — although this feels a little like snatching at straws — but all that notwithstanding, it strikes me that the image of a villain without motivation, simply operating out of a spirit of evil, is a very important Shakespearean discovery.

You think it was deliberately devised by Shakespeare and not the result of any dramatic oversight?

It's difficult to say what was done by Shakespeare consciously or unconsciously — that opens up a great labyrinth — but from the post-modernist point of view, a villain is much more credible as a villain if he has been created genetically than if he is the product of education and environment. In some way, the great monsters are *born* monsters — psychologically and morally full-blown. Now if you look to the greatest literary creations — like those of Dostoyevsky in "Brothers Karamazov" for instance, the character of Smerdyakov, is more like Iago than Iago himself. An intellectual brimming over with contempt, who tosses women, children, family, everyone into the mud. Iago is full of concepts, full of dialectical language, always ready to cite parables and dispense black jokes....

He's often like an inspired chess-master, isn't he — whereas Othello is always a pawn.

Yes, and constantly tempted to play the part of the *metteur-en-scene* — you know, the director of the show. He's constantly manipulating the other characters. It's quite ironic: the master of Iago is Othello but, looked at another way, the master of Othello is Iago.

This brings me back to my question: surely the author knew what he was doing. His sympathies appear to lie with Iago as do the sympathies of the audience — because he's so amusing, so winning. Doesn't that upset the moral balance of the play? You come out of it thinking: it's much better to be clever like Iago than a dupe like Othello.

I'm not a moralist so I cannot say. But that brings to mind another point which strengthens your opinion. This is the only one of Shakespeare's tragedies in which the wrong-doer is not forced to pay with his life. Iago remains alive at the end of the play. He may be going to the gallows but there is always the suspicion that he may outwit the hangman as well. In any case, he is not killed on stage.

Iago's world-view is entirely cynical and materialistic — the opposite of Othello's which tends to be sentimental — romanticizing pomp and majesty and warfare. Do you think there's some deliberate kind of juxtaposition intended between Iago's cynicism and Othello's sentimentality?

To some extent, yes. Othello has often been described by critics as naive — someone easily 'played upon' by Iago. I read a few months back a paper by two Israeli psychiatrists on Othello. They argued that Iago employs the techniques of modern psychiatry, but to achieve reverse effects. The modern psychiatrist uses his medical technology in order to cure the patient but Iago, using similar techniques, is pushing Othello towards a violent crime.

There is an inescapable strand of racism in OTHELLO. *Brabantio and Iago both abuse Othello for his color, and there are other references elsewhere in the play. Now of course, our contemporary knowledge of racial conflict is not directly reflected in the play, but is there some sense in which the play does speak to racial issues today?*

In OTHELLO the racial problems are similar to those depicted in THE MERCHANT OF VENICE which, as you know, is thought by many to be anti-Semitic. But primarily, I think Shakespeare consciously brought together the attraction of black and white — I mean in the most basic way: the attraction of one skin-color to another.

I remember when I was quite young before the war, at a club called the Boule Blanche in the Latin Quarter in Paris, you found only black men and young very white, often very blonde, Swedish girls. And they were always to be seen dancing together and one suspected, copulating together afterwards. There's no question that this attraction between black and white exists. And from Iago's very first lines in the play, Shakespeare posits the sexual allusion between the two races. From a casting standpoint, a director could choose many different kinds of women to play Desdemona but one thing is certain: all of them would have to be white.

But looked at simplistically, or if you like from the feminist viewpoint, OTHELLO is a play about a man — not a very young man — who seduces an extremely young woman, automatically assuming that he is to be her master and that she will be subservient to him — not just faithful but *obedient* — a very old-fashioned patriarchal view of both women and marriage. If she is unfaithful or asserts her independence, he reserves the right to kill her. You have to remember that eventually Othello realizes that Desdemona *was* innocent — which plunges him into an agony of guilt — but earlier he says "Yet she must die, else she'll betray more men." Clearly from Othello's viewpoint, if she *had* been unfaithful, he would have been perfectly entitled to take her life.

Is that because what is uppermost in Othello's mind is not Desdemona or his feelings about her, but the sense of his own reputation — his image in the eyes of others. Could it be that his ego is more offended than his heart is broken?

That's a good point and one that's been stressed by other critics of the play: that Othello is not so much jealous as he is concerned with personal prestige; that Desdemona's infidelity would destroy his social position, his idealized image of himself.

Which seems to suggest that he's profoundly insecure.

Of course, apart from the natural insecurity and shame of a man whose wife is known to be cuckolding him there's also the fact of his outsiderness. At the moment, he is necessary to the Senate as a soldier — but because of that basic insecurity, the Necessary Man can, at any moment, become expendable. Because he lacks native rights in Venice, he feels insecure both as a husband and a lover? And you know, when you find people who are insecure in their professional associations, very often they have insecure personal relations as well.

Is it conceivable that Desdemona, like some unconscious kind of flirt, could be responsible for the tragedy that befalls her?

This is something I suggested almost thirty years ago when I first dealt with the play. Of course, she is not a strumpet, but in some way, she *could* be. There is some kind of discernible susceptibility in her — reflected by Iago, by Brabantio, by Cassio — which could turn her towards a brazen sexuality. If Cassio had a sexual itch for Desdemona, there is this suggestion — because of his nature and her's, because they are fairly close in age, etc, — that under certain circumstances, they could wind up in bed together. — Also there is that curious little first scene in Act Two which has been highly criticized by Shakespearean critics in which Desdemona, Iago and Cassio are awaiting Othello's arrival in Cyprus. The scene is peppered with a lot of sexual allusion and innuendo and Desdemona, you may remember, participates quite openly in these exchanges — in no way modest or embarrassed by Iago's *double-entendres.*

You very often find, don't you, that an attractive woman is aware of her sex appeal and it is that very consciousness which often provokes a certain kind of sexual discussion on the part of men — often in a lighthearted way, as in the scene you mention — but the cause of that banter is the way the woman's sexuality affects her male company. And the woman knows it — as Desdemona seems to know it. And of course, Desdemona had many suitors before Othello — so she's not exactly a shrinking violet.

As Stanislavsky said: when you are playing a character you have to look for the opposite trait — if you're playing a beggar, you must look for his princely side; if a villain, for his redeeming qualities. Desdemona, on the face of it, is faithful and virtuous and so it would seem quite legitimate to look for other traits in her which perhaps, are not so virtuous.

This also applies, in a sense, to Othello. With hindsight, Othello can be seen as a monstrous Uncle Tom figure. Here is a black man who is the leader of a white army going to battle against a lot of brown-skinned men for the sake of an established white society? When Brabantio comes to the Duke to ask that Othello be punished for spiriting away his daughter, one of the reasons the Duke and the others hesitate is that they need Othello for the upcoming battles against the Ottomans? Is this not a political factor in what is usually considered to be a domestic tragedy?

I am partly convinced by what you say because, you know, in many of the great tragedies — as in HAMLET, for instance, the personal problems are inseparable from the political ones. Here the status of Othello is directly connected with the political problems of Venice, the war against the Turks, etc. And also, as I've said, there's the fact that he's not a general by natural ascension, but a general chosen, as it were, from abroad.

If people were not very interested in OTHELLO *as a domestic tragedy and preferred to view it entirely as a political work, do you think the play would lend itself to such an interpretation?*

That would be a problem. We know that it was during the Restoration period, and later throughout the 18th century, that the play was largely domesticated — It was not intrinsically a domestic tragedy, but the esthetics of the 18th century virtually transformed it into one. It was pitched towards melodrama and of course, the subjects of such plays are invariably a jealous husband and an innocent wife unjustly accused of infidelity. As far as the characters and the plot are concerned, you have the makings of a domesticated tragedy or melodrama. And in this dispensation, the politics of Venice, the situation of the 'stranger', the military background are entirely subordinated. By the way, this cosy 18th century view of the play is confirmed by the extant drawings from the Kean production where, for example, we see Desdemona in her bed wearing a nightcap.

Are you saying then that this was not the case in the 17th century?

No one knows with any real certainty how this play was perceived in Shakespeare's own time. After the Restoration, however, we know it was one of the most frequently revived of Shakespeare's plays with a strong emphasis on its domesticity. The question of Othello's color and the politics of Venice were not very important and the play's resolution was closer to what we think of as a 'happy ending'. Justice is vindicated; Othello's heroic stature restored by means of an heroic suicide; the villain taken to the rack; Desdemona, exonerated of any wrongdoing. — The basic structure of melodrama is meticulously observed. In the first part, the hero is manipulated or trapped by the villain but at the end, the villain is unmasked and punished and the heroine justified or rehabilitated. — But of course, for us, this kind of domesticated drama, particularly after the romantic revolution and the developments of 20th century drama, is less interesting than OTHELLO viewed as a political drama or a play about color.

Is that why contemporary directors are continually trying to expand this play, turn it into something more than it is. Because, you know, you mentioned OTHELLO *in the same breath as* KING LEAR *and* HAMLET *and I wonder whether it is really in the same league?*

I believe it is, although, as I've said, I find myself in agreement with Bradley's verdict that it is great theatre but not necessarily great tragedy — and this connects with my second view, that the stage is not necessarily the most appropriate medium for 'OTHELLO'.

Is there another medium better suited to OTHELLO?

This quality of false pathos, which is to be found in OTHELLO inclines it towards that medium in which the hero is an heroic tenor capable of scaling the highest summits of Othello's agony, through music. In opera, there is something you could almost call 'operatic justice' — which is akin to poetic justice — whereby the tenor is often expected to commit suicide, the soprano to be the innocent victim, and the baritone, the villain. The story fits quite naturally into the operatic medium. It is not an accident that the greatest success of OTHELLO in the past one hundred years, has been Verdi's 'Otello'. Opera is a natural medium for bathos — and there is some element of bathos in OTHELLO that lends itself to opera.

Is this because, even as a stage-play, it has the constituents of an opera?

In a sense, in its theatrical form, it is already a libretto for opera.

SHAKESPEARE'S OUTSIDERS

Lecture given by Marowitz at the International Shakespeare Conference in Valencia, Spain — April 22nd, 2001.

In his book THE SHIFTING POINT, Peter Brook writes that whereas other writers merely 'interpret reality", what we get from Shakespeare is not simply his "view of the world, it's something that actually resembles reality." Other artists may interpret reality, says Brook, but "what (Shakespeare) wrote is *not* interpretation, it is the thing itself."

This idea, enlarged and aggrandized, reappears in Harold Bloom's recent book "Shakespeare: The Invention of the Human" in which Bloom argues that human character as we know it, was not simply observed by Shakespeare but actually invented by him: Shakespeare, not so much an artist reflecting the world around him, but an avatar creating the prototypes that eventually become sentient human beings.

If we are to buy Professor Bloom's theory of Bardic Creationism then we must believe that there were no brooding, young intellectuals before Hamlet; no obsessive, career-driven women before Lady Macbeth; no arrogant, foolhardy old rulers like Lear commanding love from ungrateful off-springs. No wheedling, vengeful moneylenders before Shylock; no cynical, scoffing soldiers before Falstaff; no young men as besotted with juvenile love as Romeo or young girls as delirious with passion as Juliet. That all the variety of types depicted by all of Shakespeare's predecessors — Ovid, Homer, Chaucer, Spenser, Plutarch, Cinthio, Bocaccio — were simply laying small insignificant eggs that Mother Hen Shakespeare actually hatched.

I have a deep affection for Mr. Bloom and believe that as a critic and a scholar, he brings an intelligence to the canon which is titillatingly insightful and often profound. Like a brilliant and eloquent docent, he shows us around the many wings of a fascinating old castle dropping pearls-of-wisdom and rubies-of- perception wherever he goes. — But academics have a strong tendency to overstate their case — sometimes to the point of absurdity and, although I am mightily impressed by Bloom's galaxies of insights, I find his central thesis preposterous.

Now why do I begin in this narky, sardonic way bad-mouthing a highly esteemed Shakespearean scholar who has given me, and I'm sure you as well, innumerable hours of pleasure and stimulation. — Mainly as a caution to myself for what I am about to say about two of Shakespeare's plays THE MERCHANT OF VENICE and OTHELLO, may strike those that hear it as just as fanciful and absurd as Bloom's thesis strikes me. I am openly acknowledging that curious sport in which we're all engaged here; a kind of theatrical balancing act which juggles theories, hunches, insights, propositions, analyses, paradoxes, paradigms, aberrations and delusions. — In short, the traditional claptrap of Shakespearean criticism.

Only *now*, having made my disclaimer, or if you like 'Surgeon-General's Safety Warning', do I feel I can commence.

THE MERCHANT OF VENICE is not a play about money, venture capitalism, Judaism, Christianity, social justice, nuptial lotteries or Shakespeare's hang-up with Marlowe's JEW OF MALTA. It seems to me to be a play in which the author tries to balance three incompatible styles: Romance, Comedy and Tragedy.

The nuptial lottery, Bassanio's quest to win Portia, Antonio's deeply-rooted affection for his wastrel friend, (touchingly reciprocated by Bassanio) and Portia's partiality to this impecunious adventurer, is where the Romance is lodged. The Comedy grows out of Shakespeare's depiction of a stereotypical 16th century Jewish usurer who sees people almost exclusively as property (a blindspot that extends even to his daughter), and the quiz-show of the Three Sealed Boxes as performed by Portia, Nerissa and the three male contestants who seek her hand; a kind of Renaissance version of 'Who Wants To Marry a Millionairess!'

The Tragedy of course is rooted in the play's Trial Scene in which Antonio's life is imperiled by a tenacious plaintiff who, demanding that the Court apply the letter of the law, is unaware that the law is not graven in stone but etched in tablets of clay which can either bend or break depending on who handles them.

Forbidding the spillage of a drop of blood in a forfeit which permits the cutting of a pound of flesh (Portia's brilliant trump-card) is one of those legal anomalies so dear to professional attorneys which, to everyone else, seems only to make a nonsense of the law; the equivalent of a dimpled-chad which disqualifies an otherwise legitimate ballot.

One might argue that Shylock's contract was illegal to start with as its proper execution would necessarily violate a slew of other standing laws like those against Mayhem, Grievous Bodily Harm or Conspiracy to Commit Murder. But theoretically the bond entered into between Antonio and Shylock was sanctioned and certified by the State or the case would never have come to trial in the first place. So bloodthirsty as it may seem to us, it was deemed legitimate within its own social context. If that is so, to contravene it by suddenly applying another statute that nullifies it could be construed as a cruel anomaly, entrapment or simply playing fast and loose with the whole concept of the law. Striking down one law in favor of another that appears to contravene it is, at the very least, a case ripe for review by a Court of Appeal. But the Venetian court, despite its lip-service to impartiality, is clearly prejudiced against the plaintiff and will go to any lengths to foil his suit — even permitting a young, foreign whipper-snapper-of-a-justice to turn its statutes on their head.

The tragedy then is that the law, as practiced in Venice, is not impartial but prejudiced against the Jew as later laws throughout Europe unquestionably were, and as American laws were against blacks from the birth of the Republic right up to the present day.

Without meaning to reopen old political wounds, the preferences of the Florida legislature as expressed in the presidential election of 2000 were just as clearly prejudicial to the claims of Al Gore as the Duke's court was to Shylock. There too a plaintiff, but of the wrong political suasion, was perceived as an 'outsider' in regard to the prevailing political sympathies of the judges that presided over that court; so much so that they were prepared to find for his opponent whatever the official verdict might have been. A majority of the highest court, the U.S. Supreme Court, perpetuated that prejudice by refusing to permit a recount that might have produced a result inimical to their partisan preferences. Judges and attorneys have always manipulated the laws and laws have been created in such a way that they lend themselves to being bent in whichever direction clever attorneys find it possible to bend them. Fortunately, there are so many laws that one can blithely be used against the other, as it was in Shylock's case, to achieve the desired end of a ruling faction. Some call this democracy at work; others see it as the smirking, unacceptable face of Democracy or as a glaring demonstration of H.L. Mencken's aphorism: "Democracy is the theory that the common people know what they want, and deserve to get it good and hard!"

The law, as we see over and over again, is never absolute and almost never impartial. It has biases built into it because of the nature of the people who are wielding it. It is a weapon in the hands of those holding power to favor its friends and punish its enemies. Being man-made, it suffers from the moral flaws and egoistic prejudices of its creators. It is precisely because judges *are* mortal men and women that they wish to appear as emissaries of some divine power. That's why they disguise themselves in wigs and gowns, prop themselves up behind high benches, surround themselves with Roman columns and preside beneath ceilings which proclaim gold-embossed moralistic platitudes. They would have us believe they are more prescient and more omnipotent than ordinary mortals who feel human surges such as spite, vindictiveness, rancor and vengeance. Being Talmudic rather than worldly, intellectual rather than practical, Shylock fatally misreads the intentions of the Court. The fact is Shylock, by being a Jew in a Christian community, is already guilty and if he were half as bright as his clever badinage in the Trial Scene, he would have realized it and never brought a case which, no matter what its rights in law, he could not possibly win.

Ultimately, it's the Tragedy in MERCHANT which overwhelms both the Romance and the Comedy — so much so that in that last lyrical scene (Act V) we cannot possibly concentrate on the amusing squabbles of the four newly-weds because some part of us cannot shake the image of Shylock being stripped of his Jewish gabardine, his Star of David roughly replaced by a crucifix and a copy of the New Testament.

The aftermath of Shylock's tragedy highlights the fact that Shakespeare has failed at blending his three selected elements of Romance, Comedy and Tragedy into an organic whole. He commits the same mistake in MEASURE FOR MEASURE where the sexual collisions between Angelo and Isabella subvert all of the

Duke's ingenious acts of stage-management. It doesn't matter how resolutely this so-called 'comedy' resolves itself with the forced marriage of Mariana and Angelo and the equally forced marriage of Isabella and the Duke. No arbitrary nuptial resolutions can obliterate the rancid taste of Angelo's corruption of power or the nun's realization that the world is not filled with beatific angels like Saint Clare but lustful sinners like Angelo and Lucio.

They are often referred to as 'problem plays', but critics rarely identify what the problems are. Essentially, they represent a stylistic imbalance which the playwright, try as he may, cannot reconcile — which is why directors revive them over and over again trying in their productions to resolve the contradictions the author was *unable* to resolve. That may well be the underlying *raison d'être* of all revisionist Shakespeare productions. Paradoxically, it is the plays' deeply embedded imperfections that are responsible for some of the most imaginative productions of them that we occasionally see. Directorial ingenuity and the acumen of talented actors compensating for a playwright's failings: one of the best kept secret in the theatre.

* * *

If Shylock is the black sheep of the Venetian community, what are we to call Othello, that other great misfit from the same city?

One might argue that as a hired mercenary and successful warrior, Othello provides an invaluable service to the State. But then, in a much less conspicuous way, so does a moneylender. The one fortifies the city's walls; the other its economy. Shylock and Othello are both outcasts in Venice, but so long as they can provide monetary or military services, they are tolerated and grudgingly accepted.

Apart from their race and their both being war heroes, there are no striking parallels between Othello and General Colin Powell, the American Secretary of State, and yet they are both united by a painful contradiction.

Othello provides his skills and military expertise in order to wage war against a brown-skinned enemy, the Turks, who threaten the security of the State. Powell is a member of the ruling Washington elite in a democracy where he is well aware that blacks are often disenfranchised, economically disadvantaged, discriminated against and racially profiled. He sees no contradiction in belonging to a party which many blacks view with suspicion and some with open contempt. Perhaps he justifies his role in the cabinet by arguing that, he is in a position to enhance the lot of his people. Anything that shows able and effective black citizens rising to high office and being effective there, helps to remove the inequality which is embedded in the nation's shameful history, and must be counted as a virtue. Powell, by no stretch of the imagination 'an outsider", becomes an exemplar for others of his race.

Othello is not so motivated. He is an outsider who pretends he isn't and indulges in no advocacy for Moors, Turks or any other minority excluded from the seats of power. He eagerly enters into alliances against members of his own race. His services are bought and paid for and their value is openly acknowledged by his paymasters who see it as a good bargain. He knows better than Montano, Brabantio, Ludovico or the Duke how to fight battles and rout the enemy, and he knows his *paymasters* know it, and that gives him a certain grandiosity which is discernible in his manner, in his bearing and in his language. Othello is like the obnoxious CEO that all the shareholders will regularly vote to maintain in office because he consistently increases the value of their stock, and ultimately, that is what really counts in a corporation *or* in a government.

But should he lose his usefulness, should he become volatile and unpredictable, so emotionally unstable as to create doubts about his efficiency, then his 'outsiderness', invisible when efficacious, becomes a serious liability. If not a victorious warrior then Othello is nothing. When his "occupation's gone", Othello is himself a goner. (How ironic that after his downfall, it should be the crapulous and unstable Cassio who should rule in Othello's place in Cyprus. It seems to me to confirm the inherent corruptions of the Venetian government that Othello seems so proud to serve.)

The prejudice against Shylock the Jew is very thinly veiled; openly alluded to both by Gratiano and Antonio. But apart from Brabantio's indignation at losing a daughter and Iago's natural, barrack-room slurs against black-skinned men, Othello is respected. That is his power-to-deliver-the-goods is not in question and so his 'outsiderness' never becomes an issue. But it is always one in Othello's mind and, for that reason, Iago easily kindles the fires by which his general is ultimately consumed. It is Othello's own deep-rooted fears that feed those flames.

The General is aware that he has intruded into alien territory by acquiring Desdemona. This is not simply another plume on his crest, another medal for bravery-in-action. This is an incursion into a world where, hitherto, he has been a tolerated outsider. A world into which no Moor, ever before, achieved such eminence. It is his knowledge of that fact, moreso than any suspicions planted by Iago, which prevents him from consummating his marriage. Some part of him readily believes that Cassio or another member of Desdemona's race could blithely cuckold him because, endemically, they belong to the charmed society in which he is only a hired mercenary. Iago has it easy; his work is done for him by Othello's deep-rooted suspicion that a white woman will never remain faithful to an outsider. His desire to strangle her is part-and-parcel of his perceived inability to possess her, and because in the dark and rumbling boiler-room of his soul he doesn't believe he ever truly *can* possess her, the hint that someone else *has* comes springingly to the fore.

After the murder of Desdemona and the discovery of Iago's treachery, Othello reverts to these deep-seated fears and suspicions. "I am black and have not those soft parts of conversation that chamberers have". He knows that the thought that fathered his wife's murder was not spawned by his Ancient but by himself. His effusive love for Desdemona, as expressed in Act II Scene 1 when he reunites with her in Cyprus, exists to compensate for his doubts and fears about invading the Magic Circle to which he does not truly belong. "O my soul's joy" he exclaims, "If after every tempest come such calms/May the winds blow till they have wakened Death." And then: "If it were now to die/ 'twere now to be most happy; for I fear/My soul hath her content so absolute /That not another comfort like to this Succeeds in unknown fate." ......And later: "Sweet powers!/ I cannot speak enough of this content; it stops me here *(touching his heart)* It is too much of joy." And then before the entire assembly, he kisses his bride.

Othello's mode of expression with Desdemona brings to mind the effusive exhibitions of love and endearment often found between eloping married couples that, within months, are initiating divorce proceedings against one another. An histrionic display of excessive affection is always inspired by deeply grounded fears of its dissolution, as if the 'show of love' were a tonic that helped strengthen lovers' shaky sense of insecurity.

Iago's indignation at being passed over in favor of Cassio, was a convenient hammer with which Othello could confront and ultimately bludgeon that sense of wrongful intrusion that haunted him from the outset for appropriating the forbidden Desdemona to himself.

Forced to defend himself before the dignitaries of Venice, Othello says:

> "Rude am I in my speech
> And little blessed with the soft phrase of peace,
> For since these arms of mine had seven years pith
> Till now nine moons wasted, they have used
> Their dearest action in the tented field;
> And little of this great world can I speak
> More than pertains to feats of broil and battle;
> And therefore little shall I grace my cause
> In speaking for myself."

Royal lineage notwithstanding, he admits he is a man that doesn't speak the same language as those in his immediate social milieu: a prisoner-of-war then "sold to slavery", surviving in caves and empty deserts — now in the midst of Dukes, Senators, Officers and Gentlemen. And not engrossed in military or political matters but defending himself for having stolen away a Senator's daughter. How can he help but feel odd man out in such a situation and in such a society?

Shylock's loss of Jessica to Lorenzo is something akin to Othello's sense of betrayal in regard to Desdemona. In both instances, the characters' pain is commingled with a realization that an alien world has punished them for attempting to intrude upon it. Both have been punished for trespassing into a society to which they were not born. Shylock's response is vengefulness. He knows his enemies and tries to rout them using their very own weapons; the machinations of the law. Othello's is self-referential. In order to wreak *his* revenge, he must inflict punishment upon himself.

One of the hardest tasks for an actor playing Othello is how to make the transition from being head-over-heels in love with his new wife to rapidly suspecting her of base infidelity. After their loving reunion in Cyprus, there are only two short scenes before III/3 in which Othello's loathing of Desdemona's betrayal begins to fester. One moment he is besotted with his "fair warrior" and the next he is asking: bitterly: "Why did I marry?"

It doesn't take a very astute psychoanalyst to note that the seeds of Othello's destructive impulses were there long before Iago conjured them into being. And if one deduces from this that the patient is criminally ambivalent, it would be a mistaken diagnosis, for Desdemona is simply a surrogate for the entire Venetian world into which Othello has allowed himself to be lured. Being a soldier, he has a sure instinct about his enemy and, being a soldier, he lives in constant anticipation of his enemy. A soldier without an enemy is inconceivable, and Othello has a primordial need to seek out enemies and destroy them. Cassio is only a symbolic enemy. He is merely a representative of "the general camp, pioneers and all" who may have "tasted" Desdemona's "sweet body" and Othello "nothing known".

His real animus was not so much against Cassio but his own untenable position in a Venetian State in which he felt so much 'the alien' that he construed marriage to Desdemona as some magical means of integration. This, ultimately, is what brands the play a tragedy. The whole of Othello's last speech is an attempt to exonerate his irrational murder of Desdemona by citing his valuable service to that state. "An honorable murder" as he puts it, "for naught I did in hate, but all in honor." Having been manipulated into enmity against Cassio and then Desdemona and then Iago, he has finally found his *true* enemy, and it is himself, and being a good soldier, he destroys it.

* * *

If Othello's motives are repressed, unacknowledged by the General himself, Iago's are no less so.

Since Coleridge, there has been much speculation about Iago's "motiveless malignity". But there is one underlying motive that seeps into the play from Cinthio's "Hecatommithi", the known source-material of Shakespeare's tragedy.

In Cinthio, you will recall, Iago's hatred of the Moor comes out of his frustrated desire for Desdemona. But is this motivation entirely absent in Shakespeare's play simply because it's not directly incorporated into the action? At one point, he actually says, he loves Desdemona not "out of absolute lust" but partly to feed his revenge. And when Desdemona arrives at Cyprus before Othello, his banter with her fairly crackles with *double-entendres* in which, curiously, Desdemona merrily participates.

Iago, who is constantly living vicariously, turns Roderigo into a phallic surrogate just as he will shortly try to turn Cassio into another. And what makes better psychological sense than that a man should elaborately destroy the obstacle that stands between him and the woman he lusts after — not because by removing that obstacle he stands any better chance of winning her but, simply and maliciously, out of sexual spite. 'If I can't have her — neither will you — nor will anyone else!" The age-old motive behind *crimes-passionels*! And when he is finally confronted with his crime, why doesn't Iago tell Othello and the Venetian authorities what he has already told us: 'You passed over a more practiced and worthy soldier and gave the Lieutenantship to Cassio instead.' Or why doesn't he blurt out: 'I believe you seduced my wife and so what I've done to you is nothing more than tit for tat.' No, instead he says: "Demand me nothing: what you know, you know/From this time forth I never will speak word." An obdurate, stonewalling silence, perhaps because he cannot come to grips with his own smoldering, unconscious compulsion which was the lascivious desire to possess Desdemona the way Othello had; an admission he can barely confront in himself and finds impossible to declare to others. That is an overwhelming and understandable reason for pleading the 5th Amendement; to avoid the shame of self-incrimination. — The whole of Iago's intrigues against the Moor, Roderigo and Cassio are a kind of murderous, masturbatory-fantasy stemming from a starved sexual lust which is never acknowledged, never confessed, but runs powerfully beneath the current of events.

* * *

Many writers and critics have made the point that in terms of beliefs, social and religious attitudes, Shakespeare is an Invisible Man. Was he a Royalist? A crypto-Catholic? A faithful Protestant? A Champion of the Establishment or a sly subversive? The fascination of the man is that he cannot be conclusively labeled according to his works But in his treatment of Othello and Shylock, we have to recognize that he was the first writer of his time to humanize the villainous Jew and make us feel enormous sympathy for a tormented black man. It is his humanism that is so innovative and creates those tantalizing ambiguities that make it impossible for us to condemn either a flagrant usurer or a murderous general.

So in some sense, maybe Harold Bloom *did* get it right. If not the "*inventor* of the human", he certainly held an active and prosperous franchise which remains in force to this day.

MADE TO MEASURE

Conversation between Kott and Marowitz

In Whetstone's play THE HISTORIE OF PROMOS & CASSANDRA *on which* MEASURE *is presumably based, there is a traditional dispensation of old-fashioned morality. The king returns, punishes evil and rewards virtue. In Shakespeare's work, the moral ambiguity connected to the Angelo-Isabella strand is stronger than the happy ending. Why do you think Shakespeare altered the moral architecture of the play in this way?*

It's hard to say, but PROMOS AND CASSANDRA is a very naive work, a kind of comical discourse with a happy ending. But what strikes me as significant about MEASURE FOR MEASURE is that its composition coincides, more or less, with the completion of OTHELLO. The plays are completely different, of course; OTHELLO is about the heroic fall of the great warrior but the vision of that world as reflected in this play is one of decomposition. There is no place in it for true virtue. The rewards for justice are very ambiguous — similar, in a sense, to what one finds in MEASURE FOR MEASURE.

If one looks closely at the structure of MEASURE, the first half of the play seems to presage a play with a happy ending. In the Whetsone play, the heroine's brother is killed, the girl loses her virginity, the deputy has to temporarily give up his authority and be banished — all the ingredients are leading to a story in which virtue can triumph. Crime is punished but the hero perishes at the end.

But MEASURE *goes in a very different direction. It's as if Shakespeare is deliberately trying to avoid coming down on one side or the other.*

The outcome of Shakespeare's play, when performed on the stage, is total ambiguity and this is brought about because of the lack of cohesion between the first part and the second. The first half appears to be going straight towards tragedy then we have the intercession of the Duke in his priestly disguise and the introduction of a variety of tricks — the bed-tricks, exchange of prisoners' heads and so on. Though the first part is clearly inclined towards tragedy, the second part is almost a farce.

Could this schism be construed as a fault on Shakespeare's part — the work of a writer whose natural instinct led him one way but whose commercial playwriting sense dictated that he go another?

I don't think so. It seems to me this play fits more neatly with our modern sense of ambiguity than that of the Elizabethan's. Even with the usual mixtures of genres that we often find in Shakespeare — comedy, tragedy, tragi-comedy, etc, — MEASURE is almost unique in producing this kind of ambiguity — one could almost say, inconsistency.

Isabella is a heroine and, at the beginning in any case, represents a kind of idealized virginity, but she often comes across as hateful. It would appear that she doesn't understand her body or her soul; she is the implacable logician. She doesn't understand whether or not she is attracted to Angelo or even whether Angelo is attracted to her.

Do you find any indications in the text that Isabella is attracted to Angelo?

You have to bear in mind that in this play, psychic truth is hidden both from the audience and in certain cases, from the characters as well. Take the Duke, for example. Is he a priest? a believer? a non-believer? a cynic? an idealist? a madman? No one can be absolutely certain. He speaks a lot but he rarely opens his soul in any way that can be verified.

Angelo's situation in the play makes him out to be a hypocrite and so he is obliged to be deceitful. Whether he's a libertine or a lecher or simply an excessive Puritan, no one is quite sure — although we do know that he behaved like a swine in regard to Marianne.

But Escalus's references to Angelo suggest that he is extremely honorable. He says: "…his life is parallel'd/Even with the stroke and line of his great justice./He doth with holy abstinence subdue/That in himself which he spurs on his power/To qualify in others, were he meal'd with that/Which he corrects, then were he tyrannous/But this being so, he's just."

That is Escalus' opinion, but we know that Angelo promised to marry Marianne because he thought her to be a rich woman but, when she lost her dowry, abandoned her. His behavior in that case was certainly not honorable.

But sexually, morally, as far as we know, he is absolutely straight.

As far as we know — but you have to remember that in this play, while the central characters are moving about in this ducal foreground, in the background there is this twilight world of Vienna — a debauched and corrupted city. A background which does not exist in Whetsone's PROMOS AND CASSANDRA — a play without the same kind of realism as MEASURE. In Shakespeare, we are never allowed to forget that we are dealing with a city that is teeming with debauchery, syphilis, brothels, pimps — a thoroughly dissolute society.

Do you find a parallel with the world depicted in MEASURE and Shakespeare's own society?

Certainly because as always in Shakespeare, all his foreign locations, — Denmark, Vienna, Venice, etc are always England. Vienna, like London under King James, was also a society racked by hypocrisy. There is no other Shakespearean play in which the plague of syphilis is quite so strong. Everyone here is, in some way, infected with it.

Look at what happens in the main action? The hypocrisy of Angelo, the ambiguity of the Duke, Isabella's commitment to the cloister because of some opposition between her body and her soul — Angelo, Isabella, Lucio, The Duke — they are all living in a world of bordellos — a world surrounded by sick sex. Without this background, it would be impossible to understand the motion of the play. Angelo is ostensibly virtuous, as is The Duke of course, but no one can be sure that The Duke himself doesn't patronize the red light district, as Lucio in fact implies when he is talking to the Duke in his friar's disguise.

But is it only a world of sexual dissolution? There are clear references to social disturbances as well: laws not obeyed, agitation among the populace, dissatisfaction with the authorities?

Quite right, because in Shakespeare, sexual disorder often goes hand in hand with social disorder. Here you find both sex and power, out of proportion, out of balance. The law in this society is either too strong or too weak. To punish lechery with execution is disproportionate. But before the institution of this law, things in society were too lax. Before Angelo took over, things were too lenient. After Angelo assumes power, things are too excessive. Either way proper measure is not observed.

Take sex — which in this play is constantly bound up with disease — that too, is out of proportion. Being a virgin cloistered away in a monastery is too great a denial of sex. Disproportionate! So what I am contending is that Vienna, as depicted in this play, is a town entirely 'out of measure' — things are either too much or too little. Everything is out of balance.

What do you think Shakespeare is trying to say through portraying this lack of balance?

He is saying that to go from one extreme to another can produce only catastrophe. That in the real world — and Vienna is being used here as a symbol for 'the real world' — if women are either virgins or whores then womanhood itself is out of balance.

If we tried to divine a moral message from MEASURE FOR MEASURE, I think it would be utterly ironical and pessimistic. 'There is no way out.' 'The state is as rotten as it is in Denmark.' The Duke is trying to restore order; he is, as it were, the agent of order. He wishes to assert morality, punish offenders and reward the virtuous — and yet his behavior too is eccentric and unbalanced — pretending to be a monk, breaking the sacrament, divulging holy confessions to others, operating as a pimp between Marianne and Isabelle, falsifying evidence with the substitution of Ragazone's head for Claudio, and so on.

At the end of the play, isn't Shakespeare is trying to create a balance out of all these unbalanced elements?

But if we view the play head on, it is one puzzle after another. Nothing can be taken at its face value. No sooner is something said than it's contradicted.

Even the ending?

The ending in particular! Because if justice is to be done, Angelo has to marry Marianne as he had promised to do. Subsequently, through the Duke's stratagem, he slept with her and according to Elizabethan law, once the marriage has been sexually consummated, it is legal. Earlier Angelo had promised to marry her but, because they hadn't slept together, it was not considered a true marriage. But now when the Duke is asking Angelo to marry Marianne, he is meting out a proper justice.

Isn't that then restoring the equilibrium of things?

Let's go slowly here. The marriage of Angelo to Marianne restores a kind of proper balance — puts things, as it were, *in* measure. And yet this is also, in a sense, a kind of punishment, because as far as we can gather, Angelo hates this woman. The marriage between Claudio and Juliet banishes the unfair death penalty and brings about a restoration of justice. He promised to marry this girl; they slept together; he made her pregnant; they had a child, so there too, we see the restoration of order.

So where's the imbalance?

But we have four marriages here, not two. The third marriage in the play is the Duke's proposal to Isabella.

To which she never responds.

So now we have two ambiguities. One, a theatrical ambiguity which confronts the director of the play and the other, the actors playing Isabella and the Duke. It makes the resolution of this scene very difficult — the fact that she doesn't respond to the Duke's proposal. Does her silence denote "Yes' or 'Maybe" or "No'? Is it that she can't bring herself to answer or that she is afraid to answer; there are several possibilities.

So even though the play goes through the motions of resolving all the conflicts, you are saying the issues remain unresolved.

It's neither the restoration of justice nor morality because Shakespeare is always malicious and perverse. Throughout the play, he poses a maidenhead as the price for a head. If Isabella offers up her maidenhead, her brother saves his head. Now her maidenhead is in tact right up to the end of the play but the price exacted from her is the same. Although Claudio's head has been saved, she still has to pay with her maidenhead.

By marrying the Duke.

Exactly — although now in more respectable circumstances. If we watch Isabella's progress throughout the play, we tend to say to one another: this girl simply must, at some point or other, lose her virginity! It's a given!

Now we have still to get to the 4th marriage: Lucio and the whore. The Duke says you remember: "If any woman wrong'd by this lewd fellow/ As I have heard him swear himself there's one/Whom he begot with child — let her appear/And he shall marry her." Often the play concludes with the marriage procession of the three couples, but if I were directing the play, after the formal marriage processions, I would include the farcical procession of Lucio and his whore. Lucio is, in many ways, the most honest character in the play; a good friend to Claudio, a helpmate to Isabella, cheery, affectionate, fun-loving, etc. — and yet he is punished in the most extremely cruel way — which is both immoral and ambiguous.

Is it possible to emphasize the dark elements of MEASURE *and still do justice to the romantic aspects? Does a director have to choose one or other half of this play so as to avoid a lopsided effect?*

There is this long critical tradition among Shakespearean scholars to see MEASURE FOR MEASURE as 'a dark comedy' and it seems to me to be a very appropriate critical appellation. It really is a 'dark' comedy — a 'comedy' because it resolves itself with a comic solution and 'dark' for all the reasons we've already discussed. But I don't find myself persuaded by the romantic side of MEASURE FOR MEASURE.

If we examine what actually happens on stage, at the beginning for instance where Angelo is nominated as the deputy for the Duke and the threat of execution is hanging over Claudio's head, there is nothing at all romantic in these scenes. Nothing of that romantic vision of a comedy which you often get in Shakespeare. Then we have the bordello scenes, the madam, the pimps, etc. I think this is very significant for a director approaching the play. The dark underbelly of the play is not only alluded to in the text, but, right from the start, is actually there in the action of the play.

But those early 'dark scenes' you seem to be referring to, with Madame Overdone and Pompey and Elbow — surely they were intended to be comedy scenes.

For me these scenes, although I grant you they are comic, are darkly comic. For me, they exist in the world of black comedy — not lighthearted romance.

But by the time it makes that modular shift in the middle of the play when the Duke suggests the bed-trick to Isabella, it would appear as if Shakespeare is making a cold-blooded decision to push the play into a more romantic direction.

I don't think so.

Let's go over it once more. The beginning is a dark comedy — almost like the start of a tragedy — interspersed with these black comic scenes full of a kind of gallows humor among the secondary characters. The main action proceeds directly in a tragic direction — Angelo's blackmail of Isabella — there's nothing romantic there — the attempt to deflower the neophyte nun. The romanticism begins in the relationship between Juliet and Claudio but Juliet has maybe six and a half lines — the girl with child, the boy going to be executed and so on, but it's all cut off very quickly. I don't see any romantic character here.

You don't think when Lucio has that scene in which he pretends to be a good friend of The Duke's — talking to the friar who is in fact, the Duke — you don't think the comedy then becomes more light than dark?

This is a typical scene of misunderstanding and reminiscent of black farce. It's humorous certainly, but it's black humor.

Are you saying then that the blackness persists all the way through this play?

Always with Shakespeare — especially in the so-called 'problem plays' where the mood of the play is constantly shifting — it starts to look as if the play was written by two different hands or the same man at two different periods...

Of course, there is the theory, isn't there, that Middleton wrote portions of this play?

Even on the level of the style and the quality of the poetry, there is a big difference between the first part where the language is very intense, and the second part where a lot of the dialogue becomes very pedestrian.

Lucio, as you say, shuttles between the comic underworld of the play and the ducal scenes of the haut monde. Could this be because, as some scholars have suggested, the play was corrupted by a popular comic actor who simply intruded himself into scenes, and that this was in no way Shakespeare's doing? Which begs the larger question: are we often trying to interpret not the writer's intentions but the impositions of 17th century performers?

Possibly, but it's impossible to prove it. If you look at Lucio, you see one of Shakespeare's capering comic creations. Once having created him, there may well have been a temptation to use him in unlikely places. Also, being a man-of-the-theatre, Shakespeare understood that most of MEASURE was dark, and so it was necessary to lighten it with touches of humor but, as I say, only *black* humor would be in keeping with what he had already written. In MEASURE, the humor is almost always ironic.

Some critics have associated the Duke with King James — others with some other kind of deific, god-like figure. Do you find any evidence for assuming that Shakespeare intended any symbolism in the character of the Duke?

Being a critic and not a scholar nor historian, I don't usually think in those terms, so it's difficult to answer that question. But one thing is fairly obvious: King James was thought of and referred to as The Vicar of God and of course, James played this part very fastidiously. It seems to me very probable that Shakespeare was in a delicate situation in regard to this character because, in the audience's mind, there was an obvious parallel between King James and The Duke, but it was not in Shakespeare's nature merely to compose a piece of idolatry. On the other hand, he couldn't imply that the Duke was obsessed with sex, a hypocrite or an incarnation of the devil.

To my mind, the incongruity that Shakespeare had to deal with here was both to suggest, and at the same time deny, the Duke's resemblance to King James. If you imagine the first night of MEASURE FOR MEASURE, it is hard to believe that an audience would not have identified the character of the Duke with that of their monarch.

The Duke is, as you and others have said, a kind of puppeteer, stage-managing the action in order to make things come out right. He is cruel to Claudio about to be executed, and to Marianne whom he inveigles into a sexual plot which we know is contrary to Angelo's own desires; and he is cruel to Lucio whom he forces to marry a whore or be beheaded. — How does one reconcile the Duke's cruelty with what appears to be a comedy. Is this something in the playwright's nature intruding?

The Duke may be, as one of my Hungarian colleagues suggested in a recent paper, simply a madman. It may not have been the author's direct intention, but the role is filled with so many inconsistencies, a director or actor approaching it might be excused for seeing it that way. Like a pimply teenager, he seems to have a weakness both for smut and practical jokes. Someone unable to understand his own impulses, someone not yet centered. Let me put it this way: would you like to have dinner with the Duke?

Perhaps a quick pint at the pub — although it's highly unlikely I would ever find him there. — But let me push on to something else. The law that declares that fornication outside of marriage must be punished with death is very extreme. I know this originates in Whetsone's play, but could it be there was something in Shakespeare's own time that conjured it into being — a puritanical wish to punish promiscuity?

There was no law in early Jacobean times that was equivalent to the severity of the law against fornication described in MEASURE. And of course we have to remember that the Globe itself was surrounded by bordellos and in the theatre itself, there would have been a vast number of whores plying their trade.

All we can assume is that Shakespeare despised Puritanism — certainly his treatment of Malvolio would suggest that. In plays like THE TEMPEST and THE WINTER'S TALE, one detects some very dark psychic impulses that could not have been alien to Shakespeare himself. If, for instance, you look at the jealousy in THE WINTER'S TALE or in OTHELLO, the possessiveness of a character like Prospero — even towards his own daughter, there is something there that you cannot describe as 'light-hearted'.

If you had to make a deduction based on what we know from these plays, would you conclude that this playwright has a nasty, even malevolent streak in his nature?

I deny such a conclusion because in terms of verifiable knowledge about the man, what we know is so minimal. On the other hand, we are fully aware that of all the writers of that period and beyond, Shakespeare is the greatest genius the literature has produced.

Therefore, biographical analyses of that sort are simply childish and get us nowhere.

Many people dislike Isabella intensely and cannot sympathize with a young novice who would retain her chastity at the sacrifice of her brother's life? What do you feel about this?

I'm not quite sure how firmly I can assert this, but to my mind, our reaction to Isabella's decision, in the framework of the play, is somehow unfair. Some part of us insists she should go to Angelo's bed and save her brother's life.

But staunch Catholics in the audience would probably side with Isabella and understand her moral dilemma.

I would guess that, given her situation, Isabella would be very easily absolved. After all *in extremis*, it is much easier to be absolved of a sin of this kind — especially if the objective is to save a human life.

In fact, Claudio uses this argument on his sister when he says: "What sin you do to save a brother's life/Nature dispenses with the deed so far/ That it becomes a virtue."

If we regard Isabella's conflict in the light of common sense, we have to conclude that her behavior is contemptible. To enable the audience to feel the proper compassion in the performance of this play, there has to be some kind of natural attraction between Angelo and Isabella. In one moment, Angelo sees that Isabella is both a woman and a virgin and there is clearly something perverse in him that prompts him to seduce such a woman. But when Isabella, after rejecting Angelo's advances, goes to see her brother in prison, the violence of her reaction in this scene is only explicable in terms of her being attracted to Angelo.

So you believe in performance, there ought to be a visible attraction between Angelo and Isabella?

Because I notice, particularly among audiences who do not know MEASURE FOR MEASURE, there tends to be an expectation that Isabella will wind up with Angelo.

Perhaps because after a diet of so many Hollywood films, one simply expects the 'leading man' to wind up with the 'leading lady'. Should the fact that Claudio who has been living in sin with Juliet, affect our conception of Isabella and her obsession with piety and chastity? It seems as if wherever we find a dutiful daughter, she is often linked to a lecherous brother — as in the case of Ophelia and Laertes. Is there something intended in the fact that Claudio, who is thick with Lucio, is something of a debauched character whereas his sister is depicted as his moral opposite?

It's hard to say. Of Juliet, we know very little. She has very few lines and it would appear that Shakespeare was not very interested in this character.

But we know that Claudio is very much part of Lucio's world. They are good friends. Which seems to imply that Claudio lives in the play's moral twilight zone while his sister seems to inhabit the higher realm.

It's very hard to fill in the lacunae in Shakespeare's work. We know few things for sure. We know that Angelo is depicted by Shakespeare as being morally reprehensible; as villainous as he can be. We know, for instance, that Claudio is a coward...

Why would you say that?

In the scene with Isabella in the prison — all right, it's understandable that a man would be frightened to lose his head — but Claudio is not thinking of his sister at all. He's not like Romeo, for instance, who is constantly obsessed with Juliet's welfare — who lives entirely for Juliet.

Could MEASURE FOR MEASURE *be a kind of Elizabethan 'commercial' for Christianity directed to a society which, like our own, was wallowing in sin? Could its standpoint be akin to the tele-evangelists who advocate a life of purity and chastity while, in their own lives, are guilty of the same kind of vices for which they admonish their congregations?*

Just the opposite.

You mean it's a commercial against Christian morality?

It's not a commercial at all. It's a play drenched with ambiguity in which Shakespeare, as it were, tried to play both ends against the middle.

People — that's to say scholars — are always complaining about the ambiguity of this play, but if the ambiguity were removed — if it was one thing or the other — it would be a much poorer play, wouldn't it?

I guess so because from our standpoint, the ambiguity in the character of the Duke — particularly as it relates to modern psychology, the notion that life is full of paradoxes and contradictions, that the Duke is many characters in one, etc — all these things makes this character very exciting. And if we think of Isabella as someone trying to deal with a ferocious repression — a woman who goes to the cloister because she cannot deal with her overwhelming sexual impulses — that too makes the character, for us, more exciting.

Angelo is depicted as a strict Puritan — just as Shylock is depicted as a debased, money-grubbing Jew — and yet Angelo's greatest crime seems to be his sexual vulnerability to Isabella's beauty and righteousness? Which is very human. Shylock's worst trait seems to be that he loathes the very people who continually show a base contempt for him. Which is also very human. Shylock, like Angelo, has redeeming qualities. He speaks feelingly about the abuses heaped upon his race and is concerned about the religious welfare of his daughter. Angelo is genuinely contrite for the sin he has committed and asks for the punishment he so rightly deserves. — Just as directors continually look for the positive qualities in Shylock's character, so it would not be hard to see Angelo as a man more sinned against than sinning. After all, his only great crime is that he has a hard-on for Isabella. Do you think Shakespeare built this leniency into his character? Was he, perhaps, sympathetic to Angelo's plight — or do you read him as impugning Angelo for moral flaws?

I believe that the comparison between Angelo and Shylock is all wrong. First of all Shylock is a Jew and the important thing about him is that he is rebelling against his position as a Jew, reacting against the prejudices piled upon him by the Christian community and living in a world of social and racial hostilities. Angelo's situation is quite different. He has a very promising career before him; he's been appointed to a prestigious position as the Duke's deputy.

But you just said that Shakespeare was intending to depict him as villainously as possible.

Yes, because there is no justification for Angelo's behavior — whereas Shylock's behavior is entirely justified. He is being constantly provoked. If you look at the play, it would be very easy for Shakespeare to make Angelo sexually aroused. But in all his encounters with Isabella, he is a cold fish. You see him maneuvering to seduce this girl, but you don't see him overwhelmed by passion.

I'm not quite sure of that. In his very first soliloquy after encountering Isabelle he says: "Never could the strumpet/With all her double vigor art and nature,/Once stir my temper; but this virtuous maid/Subdues me quite." And before his second encounter with her, he says" O heavens,/Why does my blood thus muster to my heart/ Making it both unable for itself/And dispossessing all my other parts/Of necessary fitness." He may be cold on the outside, but he appears to be steaming within.

You said a little earlier that it's impossible to treat Angelo's behavior with sympathy. Here is a man who has pledged his allegiance to Christian doctrines, to puritanical beliefs and practices — then all of a sudden in comes a woman who causes him to weaken his resolve. That's a very human kind of failing. Let me put this to you another way. If you were directing the play and you played Angelo as a black-hearted villain, you would produce a very unsatisfactory, even banal result. If Angelo is a villain then MEASURE FOR MEASURE *becomes a melodrama.*

In one sense you're right, and of course, this is a cardinal Stanislavskyian precept. It was Stanislavsky who always told his actors: if you have to play a villain, you must portray the most decent qualities you can find to counterbalance the villainy. So it's exactly as you said: the actor should be playing Angelo as decently as possible.

But you're saying that, in your view, Shakespeare intended to make Angelo a villain.

Because I do not see any passion in the man and I am contending that his behavior to Marianne was highly unjust.

Is it really so unfair? Here, he has a contract with a woman on the basis of a certain dowry. She loses the dowry and he turns around and says: since you've lost your dowry, the bargain we struck is no longer what it was when we made it.

He's a careerist. When he arranges to have Claudio executed after having arranged to sleep with his sister, this is his most infamous act.

But why does he do that? It would be more politic to allow Claudio to live. He must know that by beheading him, he's going to cause trouble with Isabella — and yet he does it without blinking. Why is that?

Because for Shakespeare it was extremely important to make the exchange of the heads. MEASURE is predicated, in my view, on the exchange of head for maidenhead and head for head. This is the central matter of the play — because the head stands for the penis.

Surely Shakespeare didn't think in such a symbolic Freudian way? Do you really believe that Shakespeare made a metaphorical connection between the beheading of Claudio and the loss of Isabella's maidenhead?

Obviously so. Look, in our modern idiom, we understand the word 'maidenhead' but we use it quite rarely. But in Shakespeare's day, it was common parlance.

Is there an intrinsic political significance in MEASURE FOR MEASURE? *I'm thinking of the whole business of corrupt government officials, the imposition of unpopular laws, the severity of central authority, etc.*

I don't know that one can approach the play on quite that level. First of all, the events of the play, for modern audiences, are so unrealistic or improbable — the death-penalty for fornication, etc — that's so far-fetched in terms of our own experience that it would be hard for it to serve as some kind of political innuendo.

Perhaps, but what about the part of the play that deals with corrupt officials bartering political gains in return for sexual favors — that happens all the time.

I don't think that even Polish audiences who are extremely sensitive to political allusion, the abuse of power, etc. could find much direct relevance to modern times here. So much of what happens in the play appears so incongruous and fantastic.

But is it incongruous or fantastic for a man to use his political authority for selfish ends?

In the abstract, perhaps, you could say yes, a politician, an attorney, a professor, could use his privileged position to seduce a girl — but in the particular instances of the play, I don't think that comes immediately to mind. If there's something particularly revolting in the play it's the idea of such a cruel and unnatural punishment being doled out for pre-marital sex.

This brings me to another question and I'm afraid a rather long one, so bear with me.

It seems to me that Shakespeare is very cruel to his female characters. Lavinia in TITUS ANDRONICUS *is raped, loses both arms and has her tongue ripped out. Katherine in* THE SHREW *is starved, abused, deprived of sleep and forced to kowtow to her tyrannical new husband. In* RICHARD III, *Lady Anne, after a humiliating scene of courtship, winds up marrying the man who murdered her husband. Juliet, after being tortured by love, causes Romeo to take poison and is subsequently deceived into stabbing herself. Desdemona, for all her blameless fidelity, is suffocated by her abberated husband. For loving the Prince of Denmark, Ophelia is publicly abused, driven insane and then drowned. The true-*

hearted Cordelia loses both her inheritance and her husband and is eventually hanged. — And Isabella is manipulated by The Duke, made to feel guilty by Claudio, propositioned by Angelo, involved in a contemptible sexual imbroglio with his betrothed and then promptly appropriated by the Duke without even so much as a 'by your leave'. — And yet feminist-scholars find Shakespeare sympathetic and interpret his plays positively from a feminist standpoint? — How can this be?

Are you quite sure that feminine scholars interpret MEASURE FOR MEASURE in a favorable way?

They tend to say: here is a woman who has succeeded in resisting the advances of an evil, exploitative man; a woman whose sense of purpose and integrity is so strong that she's prepared to sacrifice her brother's life for a principle. Therefore they interpret Isabella as a positive character.

I could partially agree with you. You know, in the last few weeks I've been looking at OTHELLO which, in a certain way, projects a very anti-feminist vision. Bianca, for instance, is a very sympathetic whore. Desdemona enjoys making love; she has a healthy sexual appetite, and is called a whore by Othello. So that what we seem to have here is a very anti-feminist or patriarchal vision of women being either virgins or whores. And again in MEASURE, there is a strong anti-feminist attitude that springs up among the male members of the audience. They are all tacitly saying to one another: Oh stop talking so much and go to bed with the man! Somehow all of Isabella's moral protests merely encourage the desire to see her tumbled.

What do you think MEASURE FOR MEASURE *is actually about today as opposed what it may have been about in its own time?*

For me, what is contemporary in MEASURE FOR MEASURE is its ambiguous esthetic structure. For our post-modernist appetite, there is something in the broken or flawed character of the work that is very appealing. One of the greatest values of the play is that it inspires discussion. By which I mean we can be exploring its issues and implications for hours on end and never run out of things to say.

Is the reverse true — that there are certain of Shakespeare's plays which, because they are more straightforward, less 'broken' as you say, become less interesting to modern audiences?

That may be overstating the case. Sometimes you are drawn to an ambiguous or broken play; other times, you incline towards a well-constructed work. And yet I tend to think all the great Shakespearean works are in a sense flawed. HAMLET, KING LEAR, THE TEMPEST, they're all considered, by one set of scholars or another, to be flawed or troubled or problematic. MEASURE is a rich play for scholars, for students contemplating theses, for debates or symposia. You can explore it endlessly. Nothing is ever certain. Whatever you think at one moment, you eventually find yourself thinking something else the next. Is that a virtue in a play? Yes, I think it is.

ABBY CRADEN *(Isabella) and* TIM BLOUGH *(Angelo) in the revised version of* VARIATIONS ON MEASURE FOR MEASURE *directed by Marowitz at Tygres heart Shakespeare in Portland, Oregon.*
Photographer unknown.

VARIATIONS ON "MEASURE FOR MEASURE"

This article was written for the SHAKESPEARE BULLETIN prior to the production of a free adaptation of the play at Tygres Heart Shakespeare in Portland, Oregon.

Several years ago when I was living in London, I was passing through Selfridges department store and came upon one of those cosmetic demonstrations which are occasionally held to beguile customers into purchasing beauty aids. The girl in the center of the group was extolling the virtues of a new cleansing-cream that miraculously evaporated make-up. I was, at the time, about to start rehearsals for a small Grand Guignol effort called "Sherlock's Last Case", the final stage-direction of which read: "The great detective's face, doused with acid, gradually disintegrates before our eyes." I speculated that some concentrated form of this cleansing-cream might provide a solution for this daunting stage-effect.

But the product in question, efficient for its own uses, was in no way helpful in dissolving Sherlock's splendid visage. After a few moments, I left the store en route to my theatre.

A few yards up Oxford Street, still cogitating the best way to obliterate the features of the great sleuth, I suddenly felt two burly hands catch hold of me from behind. Another pair of hands grabbed my other side, and I found myself indecorously hauled into a black maria which, as I later discovered, had been tracking me since I left the store. Feeling distinctly like K in Kafka's "The Trial", I eventually overcame shock long enough to blurt out: "What the hell is going on here?!" The bobbies, who were making themselves rather over-familiar with my person, muttered between gropes: "We're just taking you down to the station-house for a little while."

At the station, I was told that I was to be booked as a 'suspected person loitering with intent to commit an arrestable offense' under the Vagrancy Act of 1824 — in spite of the fact that no incriminating evidence was found on my person. I protested my innocence, became rude and angry, stood on my constitutional rights (momentarily forgetting they did not apply in the UK) and threatened counter-action for false arrest. If I were innocent, they taunted, what was I, a solitary male, doing in the midst of a group of women at a cosmetics display? I explained that I had a professional interest in the display but thought better of launching into a description of the rather elaborate Sherlock Holmes plot as this might create suspicions of mental imbalance in addition to those already aroused.

In any case, to make a long and harrowing story short, I had been spotted by a store-detective behaving suspiciously (also dressed suspiciously, viz. beat-up blue jacket, red shirt, faded jeans, incriminating long hair), the police had been alerted, I had been duly tailed and pounced upon.

When I explained the particulars of the incident to my solicitor, I was told that, although innocent, I must be prepared to be found guilty. I couldn't quite reconcile this irrational advice with the sober and sensible voice relaying it. It was made clear to me that because a store-detective was bringing the charge, and her job was to spot and catch felons, there was a strong possibility the verdict would go against me. The fact that I was innocent was, in some curious way, not relevant to the case.

After about six weeks of waiting for a trial, it was over in a matter of moments. I was acquitted and awarded costs. The police were gently rapped on the knuckles but, on the whole, treated with immense cordiality, the magistrate appearing to be highly solicitous of their good opinion. Irrationally, I waited for the store detective (a girl in her early twenties) who had testified against me, to come forward, admit her mistake, and apologize, but the look on her face simply said: 'Well, this one slipped through the net, now back to the hunt.'

Shortly after this episode, I was asked by a Norwegian theatre to look at MEASURE FOR MEASURE as a possible future production. When I sat down to re-read it, I found all the ambivalent attitudes to the law provoked by my case, reawakened.

I had always vaguely understood that the connection between law and justice was strictly semantic; that in fact questions of right and wrong were not material to the conduct of the law which was exclusively concerned with legalities and illegalities. The law, if you were a criminal, was something to elude; if an attorney, something to outwit; if an ordinary citizen, something to avoid. Like crime itself, it could be used to get its own way and, being a weapon, the important thing was who wielded it and to what purpose it was being used. We are all in the gravitational tug of the law — even if our greatest preoccupation is only the parking fine or the fear of losing sovereignty in the World Trade Organization.

The legal context is the furniture of the social context and we sprawl on it every day of our lives. In terms of that ubiquity, there is no escaping the law.

* * *

Deep in the bowels of MEASURE FOR MEASURE I find one of the few subversive ideas Shakespeare ever trickled out of his bourgeois sensibility: that human fragility, fragile as it is, is still potent enough to destroy the fabric of man-made law, and therefore one should not respect an institution merely because it *demands* one's respect, but only to the extent that it fulfills the ideals for which it stands.

By demanding respect, the law uses a subtle intimidation against the citizenry thereby protecting itself from criticism and exposure. The 'trappings of the law', are not synonymous with the functions of justice and, to insure that justice does prevail, it must be mercilessly scrutinized by the very people in whose name it is being imposed. In short, a healthy disrespect for the law is the best way of combating its tendency towards corruption.

The offer to direct a production of MEASURE FOR MEASURE in my own adaptation at Tygres Heart in Portland was an opportunity to revisit the play and make it say with greater clarity, what I had wanted it to say when I first worked on it some twenty years ago. This involved tampering, juxtaposition, amendment, compression and distortion — all the evil tools of the revisionist's trade. To those who like their Shakespeare straight, what follows will be anathema. Hopefully, to others it will give some clue as to the ways in which Shakespearean material can be recycled without it necessarily violating everything a 'classic' stands for.

LUCIO IN THE UNDERWORLD:

MEASURE is considered by many to be one of the 'problem plays' and the 'problem' with it is fairly clear-cut. The comedy scenes, rollicking as they may be, are painfully unfunny and, unlike other of Shakespeare's sub-plots, do not enhance the main action but attenuate it. One needs to have a sense of humor cast in stone to appreciate the strained levities of Froth and Pompey's perambulations around what did or did not happen to Elbow's wife. And when an exasperated Escalus complains "This will last out a night in Russia/When nights are longest there", the majority of the audience is tacitly shouting : "Hear, hear!".

The bordello scenes illustrate how the lower orders react to the Duke's decrees against fornication and prostitution, but those responses have already been amply indicated by Lucio and the characters in the Duke's enclave, and one would have hoped for a more colorful set of incidents from the play's proles.

Lucio is the emissary between the main action and the sub-plot. He clearly belongs to the nether-world of Vienna rather than the civic hierarchy and because he shuttles freely between Claudio, the Duke, Isabella, Pompey, the Provost, etc. I chose to make him the Chorus of the play, the character (and the *only* character) that would break through the fictional framework and address the audience directly. (Of course, in the bastardized version of Shakespeare's play, he is already doing this at great length in the form of comic asides, and the theory that Lucio's lines may have been the interpolations of a popular local comedian and have nothing to do with Shakespeare is utterly plausible to me.)

Much of what Lucio says is very germane to the issues of the play and, in the original version, he is saying much of it to the disguised Duke. Since in this version, I have dismantled the Duke's double-role as the Monk and the ring-master of the bed-trick, it was necessary to assign Lucio's sentiments to other characters (e.g. Pompey) and make the aggression towards Angelo arise out of different circumstances. In the VARIATIONS, there is the following scene between an inebriated Lucio and pissed-to-the-gills Pompey. The discriminating will be able to recognize all the lines even though they have been culled from different places.

LUCIO & POMPEY: *Seated at a tavern-table. Both half-stewed and in a quiet, boozy sulk. After a pause......*

LUCIO: *(suddenly pounding down his goblet.)* Marry, this Claudio is condemned for untrussing! — *Why* should he die!?

POMPEY: Aye, a little more leniency to lechery would do no harm. Tis a general vice and impossible to extirp it quite till eating and drinking be put down. *(He trembles at his last thought and then falls into a dark despair.)* What with the war, what with the sweat, what with the gallows, and what with poverty, I am custom-shrunk. You've heard of the proclamation?

LUCIO: What proclamation?

POMPEY: All houses in the suburbs of Vienna must be plucked down.

LUCIO: Shall all our houses-of-resort in the suburbs be pulled down?

POMPEY: To the ground. *(He falls deeper into despair.)* What shall become of me?

LUCIO: *(bucking up his spirits)* Come, fear you not. Good counselors lack no clients. Though you change your place, you need not change your trade. Courage, there will be pity taken on you. You that have almost worn out your ... eyes ... in the service, you will be considered. *(Returns to his own brood.)*

POMPEY: *(tearfully)* What shall become of me?

LUCIO: *(suddenly back on his own tack)* It was a mad fantastical trick of the Duke to steal from the state and usurp the beggary he was never born to. Some say he is with the Emperor of Russia; other some, he is in Rome.

POMPEY: *(bitterly sarcastic)* Lord Angelo dukes it well in his absence.

LUCIO: *(drawing him close to him.)* They say this Angelo was not made by man and woman after his downright way of Creation

POMPEY: *(confidentially)* Some report a seamaid spawned him.

LUCIO: *(confidentially)* Others that he was begot between two stock-fishes.

POMPEY: What's certain is that when he makes water his urine is congealed ice!

(Both men drink and re-enter their own drunken worlds POMPEY *slipping back into despair.)*

LUCIO: *(suddenly returning to his theme)* Why what a ruthless thing is this in Angelo, for the rebellion of a codpiece to take away the life of a man! Would the Duke that is absent have done this?

POMPEY: *(hotly defensive))* Ere *he* would have hanged a man for getting of a hundred bastards, he would have paid for the nursing of a thousand. *(miming humping)* He had some feeling for the sport.

LUCIO: The Duke had crotchets in him. he's not past it yet. Why, he would mouth with a beggar though she smelt brown bread and garlic. *(Drawing* POMPEY *close to him for another woozy confidential moment.)* Sir, I was an inward of his and I believe I know the cause of his withdrawing.

POMPEY: Prithee, what be the cause?

LUCIO: *(tapping his finger to his nose)* 'Tis a secret must be locked within the teeth and lips. *(Both men tap their fingers to their noses sharing the secret.)*

POMPEY: *(crumbling back into himself)* I would the Duke were returned again.

(Both drunkenly contemplate the middle-distance for a moment.)

LUCIO: *(Hot and fiery)* Why this ungenitured agent will unpeople the province with continency. Sparrows must not build in his house-eaves because they are lecherous. The Duke would yet have dark deeds darkly answered. He would never bring them to light. He knew the service, and that instructed him to mercy.

(Pause). (POMPEY *biffs.* LUCIO *turns to him, gives him cold, censorious look and the lights fade to black.)*

Lucio adopts his role as Chorus shortly after Claudio's beheading which, in this version is not faked with the head of Ragozine, but is well and truly chopped off. Angelo has just suffered a twinge of remorse about Isabella's seduction and Claudio's beheading, overheard by Lucio whose moral indignation, addressed directly to the spectators, is as close to a raissoneur's speech as an adapter dares to come. Again, the discerning eye will spot a small transplant from one of the Sonnets.

(LIGHTS discover LUCIO *who has been watching* ANGELO*'s confession with contempt.)*

LUCIO: Hark how the villain would close now, after his treasonable abuses. Such a fellow is not to be talked about withal. Away with him to prison! Where is the Provost? Away with him to prison, I say. Lay bolts upon him. Let him speak no more.

(turning to the audience, as if he were a Prosecutor)

Being criminal, in double violation

Of sacred chastity and of promise-breach,

The very mercy of the law cries out

Most audible, even from his proper tongue:

'An Angelo for Claudio, death for death!

Haste still pays haste, and leisure answers leisure.

Like doth quit like and Measure still for Measure.'

Then Angelo, thy faults manifested,

'We do condemn thee to the very block
Where Claudio stooped to death, and with like haste!'
Away with him. A bawd, A wicked bawd!
Take him hence!
To the rack with him!
Touse him joint by joint!

(Drops his vengeful tirade and looks the audience straight in the eye.)

I've been a looker-on here in Vienna
Where I have seen corruption boil and bubble
Till it o'errun the stew. Laws for all faults,
But penalties then bought and sold by weight.
One law for the lowly, errant peasant,
Another for his master. 'N' all the while
Authority unchecked, its palsied fingers
Clenched around the bribe. And thus is Virtue
Mocked and made a cuckold through the town
And Justice, like the dyer's hand, subdued
To what it works in.

BAWDS & WHORES:

There is only one mention of Bridget in Shakespeare's original play. This occurs when Pompey, being taken to prison, sues to Lucio for bail and the two-faced Lucio, making the pimp's situation even worse, inquires: "Does Bridget paint still, Pompey, ha?" In fleshing her out as a character in her own right, my only justification is that it was necessary, in a compressed version of the play which discards much of the sub-plot, clearly to establish the kind of characters that inhabited Pompey's world, and as Pompey had been singled out as the chief representative of that world, I felt a bawd without a whore was an unacceptable combination. Granted, Bridget's dialogue is cod-Shakespeare, but it is not poetry, it is prose and the general level of the prose in the play's comedy-scenes are no great Shakes (pun intended). Bridget is briefly established in Pompey's first scene.

(POMPEY *is preening himself before a standing-mirror, trying on a new foppish jacket.* BRIDGET, *his whore, enters at a trot.*

BRIDGET: Hast thou heard the news, Pompey?

POMPEY: That life is hard and there isn't an honest man in twelve but he's a liar and a scoundrel. I know it well, Bridget.

BRIDGET: Nay, that all the Houses of Pleasure are to be plucked down by the decree of him who is the Duke's new deputy. *(Hands* POMPEY *a copy of the edict, with which he proceeds to fan himself.)*

POMPEY: *(dismissing the idea)* Draff and dregs, Bridget, the city could no sooner function without its strumpets than it could without its Aldermen.

BRIDGET: Two houses are already shuttered, they say, and a third's to be plucked down t'morrer.

POMPEY: Fret not, my speckled paramour, so long as the appetite is rife, our wares will be sampled at the usual market-price.

BRIDGET: And yonder, several gentlemen of the town have been clapped in irons for diverse fornications.

POMPEY: Poxy cant and gossip! The commonwealth cannot stand without its stews, they are the pillars of our nation. — Those musty edicts have been unheeded since the Flood. Besides, the Duke would never countenance chastity in Vienna; he's far too frolicsome himself.

BRIDGET: Frolicsome 'e may be, but his Deputy frolicks only when the prisoner're on the rack or swinging from a gibbet.

POMPEY: Let me instruct thee, sparrow, in the ways of the world. *(pontificating)* Man needs recreation and the more weighty his cares, the greater be his need. Now politicans, as they are treacherers and given to pilfering more than your journeymen or 'prentices be, they need more recreation than most. Ergo: the bawdy-houses are to them what the churches be to the worshippers or the stage to the rabble. *(concluding)* So long as the State doth stand, the brothels will be their base. Ergo: so long as the gentry rule this fair, polluted land, the fleshmongers shall prosper. — It doth follow as the night the day, the spring the frost, the pleasure, the pox .

What think you of this nimble raiment, Bridget. It hangs well n'est ce pas?

BRIDGET: As well as you or I may from the gallows if these laws be given teeth!!!

(She shoves the decree into his hands and exits in a huff. Surprised by herhos tility, he nonchalantly scans the leaflet. Gradually the infor mation sinks in and then, all his coolness evaporated, he looks with growing trepidation in the direction in which BRIDGET *has exited.)*

Bridget makes a brief return when Pompey is imprisoned. It seemed only right to incarcerate the whore with the bawd since they would have both been hauled in under the same charge. Also, I felt it important for there to be a thoroughly immoral woman with whom to contrast Isabella, Mariana being excised from this text and Julietta being merely an innocent fiancé for whom birth-control techniques are unavailable. At the close, the nun and the whore meet in the prison where Isabella has been incarcerated by the punitive duke.

(BRIDGET *and* ISABELLA *in a cell together.)* ISABELLA *stark awake, sitting sullenly.* BRIDGET *slowly rouses herself from sleep.*

BRIDGET: What o'clock sister?

ISABELLA: It is well past evening vespers.

BRIDGET: I heard them not.

ISABELLA: Nor were they made.

BRIDGET: *(yawning herself awake)* Which house hath they plucked you from?

ISABELLA: *(remote)* Saint Clares.

BRIDGET: *(Beat)* Must be one of the newer stys; I know it not.

(ISABELLA *sits stonily incommunicado)*

BRIDGET: 'Tis a cruel sport to herd poor women from their trunk-work, denying us livelihood and our clients joy.

ISABELLA: (*Beat*) Surely such a life as thine can yield thee no moiety of pleasure.

BRIDGET: 'Tis better than being a scullery-maid or slicing offal in a butcher's. And for every wizened goat stinkin' o garlick and ale that topples me backward, there's often a young blade with a good leg and a sweet-smellin' breath that makes it all one.

ISABELLA: How can'st thou draw pleasure from defiled lust?

BRIDGET: If not from the coupling itself then from the bounty it brings. After all, *'tis* woman's work and has been since the dawn of time.

ISABELLA: 'Tis not God's work nor His will that you should do it.

BRIDGET: Then should He provide me with some better accompt, for God knows well, I need my food and raiment.

ISABELLA: But what of thy sins, sister? Do they not weigh heavily on thee?

BRIDGET: Only when stout fleshmongers mount my foc'sle, sister, then am I near pressed to death. But most oftentimes tis speedy work as men do not tarry when their business's done.

ISABELLA: Hast thou no friends or kin to tend thy needs?

BRIDGET: I have Pompey, but he's more fop than friend. These past two Whitsuntides, I had me a husband, and a more poxy varlet there never was. He made mushroom pies of both me eyes, broke me spleen in three places, then pilfered away my little store of savings a'fore he went off to fight the wars in the Low Country.

I'd as lief have a hasty client than a skulking brute like that. And how many wives are there that suffer worse offences and daily bless the bliss that hold's 'em captive? — Whorin's no frolick, but it's better'n marriage when marriage is a misery.

ISABELLA: Dost thou not fear damnation, thy soul being imperilled?

BRIDGET: I fear more my belly being empty and my throat parched. But yieldin' favours' not all miltch and misery, sister. There's *(gruffly)* men and there's *(appreciatively)* men. And when love and lust are both commixt, there's sometimes heaven 'neath the sheets. 'N sure you've known it so yourself?

(ISABELLA *says nothing.*)

With some stripling youth or t'other?

(ISABELLA *says nothing.*)

Have you not??

(BRIDGET *peers into* ISABELLA'*s face anticipating some reply.* ISABELLA *is painfully quiet as the Lights Fade Out.)*

SEXY NUNS:

In George Whetsone's PROMOS AND CASSANDRA which, along with shreds from Cinthio, provided root-material for Shakespeare's MEASURE FOR MEASURE, Cassandra (the Isabella-figure) actually has intercourse with Promos (the Angelo-figure) and when he is condemned to be beheaded, Cassandra discovers that she genuinely loves him and pleads to have his life spared. Throughout the history of MEASURE FOR MEASURE, there has always been the hint that Isabella (who, if there was ever a lady that "protests too much", it is she) might well have experienced some kind of sexual stirrings when propositioned by the proper Angelo. Not only because this was a man making a sexual overture, but the kind of man that someone like the repressed Isabella (who pleads for "a more strict restraint upon the sisterhood") would plausibly fancy. If ever a computer-date match-up worked perfectly, it was Angelo and Isabella: the former, a tight, buttoned up, cold-hearted Puritan; the latter, a self-abnegating, ascetic bride-of-Christ. We know from the mythology of convent-bred country girls who ultimately become raving nymphos that the greatest aphrodisiac of all is self-denial and Isabella is a supreme case in point.

Therefore, it is not fanciful to imagine a sexual attraction between the staid lecher and the vehemently-chaste votarist of St. Clare. Indeed, the undertone from Whetstone's play tacitly informs that relationship throughout Shakespeare's play and has been conveyed (often heavy-handedly) in several past productions. In the VARIATIONS, I simply wanted to suggest the sexual impulse that could manifest itself when two properly-matched adults find themselves in an intimate situation, even when one of them clearly repulses the advance. In one of the dream-sequences before Isabella looses herself to Angelo, the amatory aspect of that relationship is briefly intimated:

ANGELO: *(tenderly taking her round the waist)*
Plainly conceive, I love you.

ISABELLA: *(flirtatiously)* My brother did love Juliet.
And you tell me he shall die for't.

ANGELO: *(amorously)* He shall not Isabel, if you give me love.

ISABELLA: *(coquettishly)* I know your virtue hath a license in't
Which seems a little fouler than it is,
To pluck on others.

ANGELO: *(fondly)* Believe me, on mine honour,
My words express my purpose.

ISABELLA: *(playfully)* Ha! Little honour to be much believed.
And most pernicious purpose.
(teasingly) Seeming, seeming!
(She falls willingly into his arms, then mock-seriously....)
Sign me a present pardon for my brother,
Or with an outstretched throat I'll tell the world
What man thou art.

ANGELO: *(drawing her closer, playfully)*
Who will believe thee, Isabel?

(The two lovers kiss fondly. ANGELO *vanishes and a penitent* ISABELLA *is discovered kneeling before the* BISHOP *who is hearing her confession.)*

The Purists will insist the words go one way and the action another, but that is one of the glories of theatre; that sub-text can sometimes so recondition text that it becomes a dramatically-acceptable reverse-truth. Indeed, the whole point of the VARIATIONS is to tell a different story through Shakespeare's fable than the one originally intended. Again, the purists will cry, "Distortion!" but in the contemporary theatre this has become less a term-of-abuse and more an interpretational tool that requires finite qualification. Shakespeare never intended HENRY V to become a piece of jingoistic propaganda as it did in Olivier's film in the 40s, nor RICHARD III to become an anti-Stalinist diatribe as it did in the Rushtavheli production in Georgia, or a tirade against contemporary British fascism as it did in the Richard Eyre-Ian McKellan National Theatre production at South Bank. The only acid test is theatrical efficacy. Either an off-the-wall notion about a classic manages to reassimilate the Shakespearean material and produce a viable innovation, or it doesn't. When it doesn't, it deserves all the opprobrium which is usually heaped upon it. When it does, it should suggest, to the broad-minded, that "there is more in heaven and earth than is usually dreamt of" in an academic's Bardolatry.

THE BISHOP OF VIENNA:

There is no Bishop of Vienna in Shakespeare's MEASURE FOR MEASURE, but he plays a crucial role in the VARIATIONS. Underlying all of the Duke's pieties, Angelo's remorse and Isabella's chastity are biblical concepts which are regularly flouted or hypocritically affirmed. The Puritanism that Shakespeare regularly mocked and so perfectly epitomized in Angelo, is a perversion of Christian teachings.

Inspired perhaps by his monkish disguise, the Duke fires off a number of high-sounding moral sentiments, but his behavior is essentially amoral. He imposes strict decrees which are contrary to his own nature and practice (if Lucio's descriptions are to be believed), and when they backfire, he conveniently scarpers. He manipulates virtually everyone he comes into contact with. He flatters Angelo to take on a thankless task, employs Isabella in a scheme to return Mariana to a husband who has already discarded her and saddles Lucio with a whorish wife out of spite for being slandered. Toying with Isabella's emotions in regard to both Angelo and Claudio (whom Isabella believes to be executed) is both unnecessarily and characteristically cruel behavior and his blithe appropriation of the nun at the end of the play smacks heavily of *droit du seigneur*. And yet, this is the man who mouthes sentiments such as:

He who the sword of heaven will bear
Should be as holy as severe;
Pattern himself to know,
Grace to stand and virtue go'
More not less to others paying
Than by self-offences weighing.

Many of the Duke's more fulsome preachings are given over to the Bishop who, in a Viennese state run by Vincentio, exerts the kind of nefarious influence that conjures up the cunning of Cardinal Richilieu.

Upon the Duke's cruel decrees and vindictive statutes falls the shadow of a repressive Church. Its odor of sanctity clogs the nostrils of the votarists of Saint Clare and given Vincentio's merciless regime, its political dictates are invariably bolstered by holy writ. The Bishop is there because in a despotic state, the suffering of Man is invariably predicated on the wrath of God.

STORIES WITHIN STORIES:

In Shakespeare's MEASURE, the Duke, a weak-willed leader under pressure from a rebellious citizenry, abdicates his position and appoints a sterner substitute to take the heat. The Duke's execution of the law is unjust in two regards: it punishes natural sexual impulses with cruel and unnatural penalties, and installs a surrogate-authority that imposes even harsher measures on the populace. When his deputy attempts an immoral seduction of a novitiate-nun in return for sparing her brother's life, the Duke returns in the disguise of a churchman and prevents the crime from taking place by substituting a discarded former lover for the innocent virgin. When the wronged woman protests the crime, the Duke, after sadistically toying with the victim, reveals how, through chicanery and guile, he has twisted the law to reprieve the doomed brother of the innocent girl and punish the judicial malefactor by forcing him to marry a woman he does not love. As a final act of arrogance, the Duke appropriates the wronged innocent for himself (without so much as a 'by your leave') and presumably, the cruel and corrupt regime picks up where it left off. Two men (Lucio and Angelo) have been forced into unions which they find distasteful and the Duke, whose weakness initially instigated all the problems of the State acquires a bride and his regime, a new lease-on-life.

The cynicism that permeates this fable is Shakespeare's; its most fulsome aspect being the assumption that despite the many injustices perpetrated by the Duke and his cohorts, justice is somehow effectively restored.

In the VARIATIONS, Vincentio's transformation into the friar is excised and with it, the entire 'bed-trick' which makes up a large chunk of the original plot. Instead, Angelo seduces Isabella, and despite their bargain, Claudio is beheaded and his sister left high and dry. When the Duke returns, Isabella exhorts him to condemn the lying seducer and the broken contract which has robbed her of both her virtue and her brother's life. The Duke, being politically allied to Angelo and appreciative of the way he has cleaned up his own mess in Vienna, not only does not condemn Angelo, but turns on Isabella as a troublemaker who would further weaken the integrity of his government. The innocent betrayed by the Deputy is now more foully betrayed by the Duke who will not hear any calumny against his own. Isabella is hauled off to jail. In the final scene, she is released only to become the sexual pawn of all the male hierarchy that inhabit the play.

(*The* DUKE, *in a casual dressing-gown, is lolling on a couch. After a moment, he rings a small bell and the* PROVOST *arrives.*)

DUKE: Call that same Isabel here once again. I would speak with her.

(*The* DUKE *lights up a cigar, takes a puff and luxuriates on his couch.* ISABELLA *is ushered in by the* PROVOST. *She is now wearing a thin, simple shift. The* DUKE *gestures for the*

PROVOST *to leave which he promptly does. There is a long, strained silence, as* ISABELLA *waits and the* DUKE *puffs.)*

Isabella. — Are you married?

ISABELLA: *(softly and grim)* No, my lord.

DUKE: Are you a maid?

ISABELLA: *(Beat)* No, my lord.

DUKE: A widow then?

ISABELLA: Neither, my lord.

DUKE: *(lightly)* Why you are nothing then. Neither maid, Widow nor wife.

*(*ISABELLA *does not thaw out. She remains tight-lipped. He bids her to sit down on the couch. After a moment's hesitation, she does so and he joins her there.)*

As the matter now stands, Angelo will avoid your accusation; he made trial of you only. Therefore fasten your ear on my advisings. To the love I have in doing good, a remedy presents itself.

*(*DUKE *waits for he reply but* ISABELLA *sits stone-faced and silent. The* DUKE *draws closer.)*

I have a motion much imports your good,
Whereto if you'll a willing ear incline,
What's mine is yours, and what is yours mine.

*(*ISABELLA *turns to the* DUKE, *not comprehending his words.)*

The satisfaction I would require is likewise your own benefit.

*(*ISABELLA *continues to stare at him uncomprehendingly... Then, as if to make it crystal clear.....)*

You are pardoned, Isabel.

*(*ISABELLA *looks quizzically at the* DUKE, *still not sure of his meaning, and half-smiles thinking she is the recipient of charity. The* DUKE *draws even closer to her and slides his arm around her waist.)*

(quietly, hot) And now dear maid, be you as free to us.

(As the penny drops, ISABELLA *pulls away from the* DUKE *and breaks downstage. She tries to flee to the Left, but* ANGELO *suddenly appears there barring her way.*

She tries to flee to the Right but LUCIO *appears there barring that escape route.*

As she tries to escape to the side, CLAUDIO *suddenly appears barring that exit.*

Encircled by all four men, ISABELLA *is terror-stricken. She turns pleadingly to the* DUKE *who merely smiles.*

As all four men slowly begin to bear down on her, she looks fran tically from one to the other as THE LIGHTS FADE TO BLACK.*)*

What Shakespeare seems to be saying in the original play is that a measured application of justice cunningly enforced can banish evil and uncorrupt the corruptest forms of Justice. Of course, we all know better. The Law does not mete out Justice; it can just as readily mete out injustice (e.g. O.J. Simpson, Rodney King, Amadou Diallo, etc etc.) Behind its austere facade, compromises, deals and plea-bargains mock the evils perpetrated on innocent victims and there is a generally held belief that clever, high-priced attorneys have the power to alchemize Wrong into Right and regularly do so with the active collusion of the justice-system.

Our cynicism, and Shakespeare's is, in this day and age, even more widespread than it ever was in the 17th century. A woman like Isabella, alleging sexual abuse in a political set of circumstances, realizes she is entering a lion's den if she looks for vindication from the powers-that-be. The Law of the State only barely conceals the Law of the Jungle whose rigors determine all outcomes. Despite the fact that we fob ourselves off with the homily that the barrel contains only a few bad apples, the reality is, in New York, in L.A. in major urban centers throughout the country, the *entire* barrel is contaminated — so much so, that respect for lawyers is now on a par with respect for politicians — which is to say, virtually nil.

In MEASURE, Shakespeare depicts the law's corruption and then being a staunch advocate of the status-quo, window-dresses events in such a way that they produce a 'feel good' ending. Whatever Shakespeare was, he was no fiery reformer or fearless iconoclast. He knew on which side his scone was buttered. But being a true artist, he could not help but faithfully depict the corruption that festered in his society and, as is so often the case with Shakespeare, the negative factors ring truer and carry more reverberation than the marmalade-morality which he spreads over them. For me, the nexus of MEASURE FOR MEASURE is its insight into man's deep-seated malevolence; the facade, a fairy-tale about bad people getting just deserts in a world wisely superintended by a benevolent deity. And for that reason it is perhaps the most modern play in the classical reperotire.

* * *

Postscript:

(After the production of the VARIATIONS in Portland, the reaction, as always, was split down the middle. The establishment newspaper found it "inert....spare and chilly"; the critic of its leading cultural weekly who had been highly critical of the Tygres Heart theatre for many years, called it "one of the clearest and most disciplined to be seen in Portland" and concluded "This may not be Shakespeare's play, yet, strangely it's the best Shakespeare I've seen in four long, dry years." Over the years, I had grown accustomed to these extreme reactions to the adaptations and tried to prepare the company for the kind of reception it was likely to get. Innovative Shakespeare, free adaptations, gross liberty-taking-with-the-text invariably evoke the wrath of the Bard's Swiss Guard. The desire for the plays of Shakespeare to deliver the melodies and harmonies with which they were first experienced and enjoyed, is unwavering. Not to do so is like advertising a symphony by Mozart and delivering a concerto by Webern. The grating on one's nerves is almost palpable. — I sympathize.)

CUE TO PASSION:
SHAKESPEAREAN ACTING

Lecture given by Marowitz at the 5th Annual Conference of The Association of Literary Scholars & Critics in New York City, October 1999

As we all know, Shakespeare has been having a particularly good year. The film "Shakespeare in Love" has dramatically resuscitated his career — not that it was noticeably in decline. And, according to the BBC (and who would be rash enough to argue with that august body), he is the Man of the Millennium. His face is on T-shirts, crockery, calendars, shaving-mugs and, I'm reliably informed by an X-rated friend from San Francisco, dildoes as well. I understand that as a result of his bevy of recent screen credits, he is up for a posthumous Oscar. — If he felt obliged to thank all the sources from which he plagiarized his work, the acceptance speech would run disastrously overtime.

The fact is, Will has become nothing less than a Superstar and we fully expect to read tantalizing accounts in The National Enquirer about kinky goings-on in Ann Hathaway's cottage or wife-swapping at New Place, Stratford. That will unquestionably be followed by revelations about his long-standing affair with an amorous Kit Marlowe and a learned treatise in The Shakespeare Quarterly which identifies the dark lady as Thomas Kyd-in-drag. This is the downside of notoriety and since Will is on a roll, we have to steel ourselves for the worst.

But putting media-hyped imagery to one side, my purpose here today is to concentrate on the author of the plays and the men, boys and women who, over the years, have interpreted them on the stage.

In the 1950s and early sixties, scholars seriously began to speculate as to what precisely took place on Elizabethan stages. What was the character of Elizabethan acting? The discussion which rapidly became a controversy, divided people into two camps. The formalist position was firmly stated by people like Alfred Harbage who believed that, over the years, a kind of repertoire of gestures and movements had been established through the Miracle and Mystery plays and that when Shakespeare came along, the works were conveyed in the formal or representational acting-style which was prevalent at the time. The opposing view, persuasively put by critics like B.L. Joseph was that, by all accounts, acting in the 16th century was thoroughly natural and unstereotyped; that the Elizabethan actor appeared "as if he were the very man whom he represented' and the performances at theatres like the Swan, the Rose and the Globe were, to quote three of Joseph's most commonly used adjectives, "natural", "familiar" and "lifelike".

The controversy about Elizabethan acting is reminiscent of the one triggered by Diderot in the 18th century as to whether or not the actor was consumed by true emotions or operated according to a series of technical calculations. The same issues that got rehashed in the latter part of the 19th century when Coquelin and Henry Irving refueled the debate and William Archer recorded all the pros and cons in his book MASKS OR FACES: *A Study in the Psychology of Acting*.

That dispute *re*appeared in a slightly altered form in the 50s and 60s when proponents of the Stanislavsky System — or more fashionably The Method, Lee Strasberg's distortion of same — railed against the externalism of a British acting tradition which emphasized vocal technique and bodily deportment, rather than "emotional truthfulness" and "living the part".

All of these so-called controversies were in a sense, pointless; people taking up partisan positions which could be argued in only the most general terms and unprovable by any conclusive, scientific evidence. (Not that theories about art can *ever* be scientifically proven — which is what makes them so much more beguiling than chemical formulae or binomial theorems.)

Diderots' paradox concerned itself with an artificial distinction: actors who yielded to feeling and those that kept it under strict control. Any practicing actor could have told him that virtually every performance presents a compromise between both states; that an actor is constantly fluctuating between being "lost in his role" and consciously guiding it, and that this 'neither-nor' state creates a sensibility which is not subject to one doctrine or the other. — There never was an actor who didn't technically keep his emotions in check and occasionally toss himself into their whirlpool.

The fact is even so-called non-or-anti-Method actors proceed from precisely the same starting point as those that revere Stanislavsky or Strasberg. They work out the meaning of events in their head and, using trial and error, test the plausibility or implausibility of their choices, gradually developing a logic of behavior to which they ultimately commit themselves. That's what Irving, Olivier, Gielgud and Ralph Richardson did; what Paul Scofield, and Judi Dench do — none of whom would, or would have, counted themselves adherents of The Method.

The elements of those opposite ideologies — The Real or the Artificial — the Natural or the Studied — underlie the probes that modern scholars and critics have undertaken in regard to Elizabethan acting. And in a sense, their opposing views, although passionately held, are just as ill-conceived.

Acting styles in the theatre are never *a priori*; they're always determined by the nature of the material playwrights impose upon actors. The highly structured formality of Sophocles or Euripedes conjured up the pomp and ceremoniousness of what took place on stages in 5th century Greece. The rigid conventions of the Miracle and Morality plays with their doggerel rhymes and symbolic personages encouraged actors in the middle ages into a representational form of acting that reflected the nature of that material. By the time the Renaissance kicked in, changes were obviously being made. And when we get to transitional works such as RALPH ROISER DOISTER and GAMMER GURTON'S NEEDLE and playwrights are depicting recognizable middle and working class characters, the acting style is clearly going through a transition. A kind of naturalism is seeping though the formalistic writing, but the tug of older, more rigid conventions are still very much alive.

When Marlowe enters the scene, with his highly wrought, and grandiloquent diction, the actor has to jack himself up further than ever before. You can't casualize or 'methodize' lines like:

"Now clear the triple region of the air

And let the majesty of Heaven behold

Their scourge, and terror tread on emperors.

Smile stars that reigned at my nativity,

And dim the brightness of your neighbor lamps!

Disdain to borrow light of Cynthia!

For I, the chiefest lamp of all the earth,

First rising in the East with mild aspect,

But fix'ed now in the meridian line,

Will send up fire to your turning spheres,

And cause the sun to borrow light of you.

Marlowe forces actors to fill their lungs, expand their throax, quiver their tonsils and make a godawful noise that probably ricocheted around the perimeter of playhouses like The Theatre and The Rose. *That* acting style has to be large, imperious and histrionic — which in no way means hollow, bombastic or artificial. For when Marlowe saunters into Dr. Faustus' study or consorts with scholars and servants, or has a dialectical discussion with Mephistopheles about the location of hell, it's inconceivable that the grander, rhetorical style would still prevail. In such scenes, the actor has to adopt the more subdued, naturalistic tones of a man bartering his soul for immortality. Just as when Faustus' hour finally comes and he desperately seeks redemption from God, the acting style escalates again to Tamburlanian heights and we're in a mold reminiscent of the Mystery Plays which, in fact, run all the way through THE TRAGICAL HISTORY OF DOTOR FAUSTUS like a, bubbling underground spring.

The same shuttling and segues are equally true of Shakespeare who, like the inspired jazz-artist he is, moves from cool riffs to mournful blues to swinging up-tempo rhythms. The style of the scenes shift from Public to Private, from Pastoral to Domestic, from Formal to Casual — and the actor necessarily shifts with them.

The verse is constantly changing. An actor mediating the pain of a soliloquy like "O, that this too too solid flesh would melt" has to carefully mix pastel shades with exquisite subtlety in order to convey the anguish and uncertainty contained in that brooding meditation. Just as the Chorus from HENRY V has to, as it were, splash his canvas with bold, primary colors to create "the vasty fields of France" or "the very casques that did affright the air at

Agincourt". Shakespeare is constantly handing the actor different kinds of implements: charcoal, pastels, oils, graffiti-sprays, flame-throwers, grenades, — occasionally stink-bombs, and the actor is adapting himself accordingly.

All one can say with some degree of confidence is that when Shakespeare came onto the scene, he brought a certain kind of 'new naturalism' with him. But did it saturate the entire performance and banish the formalism or the rhetoric? Of course, it didn't! The plays reverberate with the plangent sounds of the earlier theatre — even as they modulate into the subtler music of what an Elizabethan might call, 'modernity'.

But none of that in any way addresses the question about what it was 16th century audiences actually saw on the stage. To get a somewhat more conclusive idea of the Elizabethan acting style, we have to examine the conditions that actually obtained in the theatres.

We know that before the advent of the so-called 'private theatres', playhouses like the Rose, the Swan and the Globe were open constructions with small fretted roofs above the actors and a certain amount of covering for the galleries, but none for the groundlings or 'stinkards' who huddled or sat in an open pit that hugged the acting-area on three sides. There were pippins, ale and hazlenuts sold to the audience. The throng contained gallants, apprentices, servants, law-students, prostitutes; a sense of lively eroticism prevailed; a sexy atmosphere; a lot of singles eying the available merchandise; a lot of horny young men 'making out' or certainly trying to. There were pick-pockets and other assorted villains who are attracted by crowds, although they tended to congregate more in the taverns than at the theatres. People smoked, chatted, horsed around. From all accounts, it was a good-hearted crowd, anxious to hear the play.

But it *was* London and it was the outdoors, and there were the vicissitudes of the weather to contend with. No passing jet-liners — but perhaps the sounds of bear-baiting and roaring crowds not too far away; probably the rumble of carts and horse's hooves just outside the walls of the theatre. And as for the performance, of course, it was acoustic — not wired for sound.

Any actor who has ever acted in an outdoor amphitheatre will tell you that a different dynamic obtains. The weather itself is a sound factor and whatever one is trying to express has to be that bit more 'projected'. Even quiet moments, intimate moments, lyrical moments, need that slight upward-tuning in order to carry to a throng of spectators fanned out in front of an apron-stage. It's the vigorous, heady, formal material that works best and there's a kind of exhilaration in enlarging one's performance to connect up with the collective sensibility of a spread public.

The maximum capacity at a theatre like the Rose was about 2500 persons. The Swan could play to 3000; the Fortune, to approximately 2340. Presumably, like all theatres there were some 'bad nights' — or, in this case, bad afternoons. But the theatre was a great novelty and a favorite meeting-place and it's quite possible, that it was filled almost to capacity for many of its performances, and since so many Elizabethans were able to quote lines from the plays, it may also have been the advent of the repeat-ticket-buyers — something the movies erroneously believe they started.

So we have to try to visualize several thousand spectators, in a largely open space, with contingent sounds both from within and without, attending to a group of players who are conveying some of the greatest subtleties ever created by a practicing playwright — in an era in which Theatre was as novel as talking-films were to us in the early thirties, or high-speed computers are today.

The actors would have *had* to enlarge their performances both vocally and kinetically, in order to convey their meanings. The circumstances militated against the kind of intimacy we associate with television or filmed close-ups. It was a theatre primarily for language but we know that formalized gesture accompanied language and we also know that the effect was utterly truthful and believable. At least it moved the spectators of its time.

Remember that what so moves Hamlet, touches Polonius and brings tears even into the *actors'* eyes, is the Player King's speech about Pyramus, Priam and Hecuba: a rhetorical chunk of epic verse which, because it so "forces the actor's soul to his own conceit" quite overwhelms the Prince and, like any evocative performance, triggers something in the listener's psyche which gives him a "motive and a cue for passion" — namely, the idea of staging a little play that parallels Claudius' alleged crime against his father. Clunky and artificial as that piece of narrative verse seems to us, it served to move its auditors, including the sensitive and well-educated scholar from Wittenberg, and, I would contend, that there's no way of performing the Player King's excerpt — except by investing it with the size and clout that highly-wrought language demands.

And so the argument for a heightened kind of acting — in all moods and to convey all states-of-being — seems to me to be incontestable. Even today, Shakespeare equals Size — no matter what the theatre and in almost every play — from the majestic formality of JULIUS CAESAR and CORIOLANUS to the domestic intimacies of OTHELLO and the sit-com inanities of MERRY WIVES OF WINDSOR. — However, every good actor understands that extending the size of a dramatic moment does not mean falsifying it — but merely spreading it wide enough for it to carry to all the house. And I would think actors like Alleyn and Burbage, Kemp and Condell understood that instinctively.

The whole history of modern acting from the early 1800s to the present is a gradual descent from the histrionic, high style to behaviorism, and every transition in between was always hailed as "more naturalistic" than the last. Edwin Booth cut down the florid style of Edwin Forrest bringing what was then considered "realism' to 19th century audiences. David Belasco, who was the disciple and secretary of Dion Bouccicault, refined the melodramatic fustian of his mentor. And it should be remembered that despite Bouccicault's treacly sentimentality and trumped-up emotions, he was *also* lauded for introducing a greater degree of realism to the stage. Still, you can see in the film-clips of Johnson Forbes-Robertson and John Barrymore that, effective as these actors must have been in the twenties, there is a patina of what we can only all 'hamminess' that clings to their performances. Perhaps 'hamminess' is the wrong word; maybe it's more like 'magnitude'. Whenever we get a strongly delineated outer-form without an equivalent inner content, we tend to disparage such actors. But we tend to prize actors such as Donald Wolfit and Laurence Olivier not for their verismilitude but for their ability to convey the grand passions in the most demanding classical roles. — Which brings us to the splendors and agonies of Shakespearean acting today.

Why is it so hard to achieve? Why are we so dissatisfied with it? Why does it seem to run against the American grain? Why are we so intimidated by the British who, it's generally conceded, know better than we do how to perform the classics?

In June of this year, Sir Peter Hall mounted MEASURE FOR MEASURE and MIDSUMMER NIGHT'S DREAM *at* the Ahmanson Theatre in Los Angeles with an almost exclusively American company. Prior to the opening of these productions, American actors were put through their paces by Sir Peter, the declared object being to teach them "how to serve the text"; that is, to discard both the peculiarities and vulgarities of casual American behavior and develop both a respect and a proficiency for the technical demands of classical language.

In meticulously projecting the language and piously observing the verse-structure, the productions turned what would commonly be a virtue, into an ongoing irritation. Many in the audience felt patronized by actors pounding every iambic and fairy-lighting every pentameter. The texts of the plays were so passionately coddled throughout that the sub-text got suffocated in the embrace. We were so carried away by stress and scansion that motive and meaning fell by the wayside. — Throughout, the Hallistic dictum that Language is Supreme and that the Secret of Shakespeare lies in the prosody was so unwaveringly obeyed that the roughness of character and the idiosyncrasies of human behavior disappeared in a mist of pedantry.

Ironically, Hall had begun this experiment with this largely American cast wanting to mine the genius of the national character of the country in which he was working. He wound up actually 'anglicizing' this company of American actors — not by encouraging them into phony British accents but by immersing them in the cloying external approach which, for decades, has been the curse of his own homeland. And he proved beyond the shadow of a doubt, that productions that remain piously true to the text but are devoid of new ideas or new connections are fundamentally unsatisfying.

The irony here is that a technical approach to verse-speaking is precisely what the American actor most lacks. But the *greater* irony is that effective Shakespearean acting is not arrived at by adhering to the principles of prosody. If you follow scansion slavishly, you can't help but produce a kind of doggerel. It's like strictly observing punctuation in a piece of contemporary prose. If you were to do that, you'd find yourself talking like a Dalek. In Shakespeare, it is Sense that determines rhythm and intention that determines stress. The verse is clay not marble and it's the actor who turns the potter's wheel. Scansion is often a good guide as to which word should be emphasized over another, but you always have a choice between three to five words, and it's up to the actor to decide where the stress should fall. And that determination comes from the nuance of his interpretation — not from a scholarly study of the origins of the verse. In short, the reciprocal imagination of both actor and director is the determining factor. Shakespeare's words are simply a means to that end.

Being paralyzed by prosody is one of the great pitfalls of American Shakespeare, the other is the tendency of actors to convey feeling that blurs the imagery or so saturates the words that the verse becomes dislocated. We all understand that with Shakespeare, it's often a matter of working backwards from the text. Instead of going from the inside out, as the Method instructs, the actor works from the outside in. Nor is this, as some people tend to believe, an external approach. The fact is it doesn't matter one whit if the relevant emotions are motivated from the language to the character or the other way round.

In Shakespeare, it's often the case that the language graphically describes the emotion. "Now could I drink hot blood/And do such bitter business as the day/Would quake to look on."/ clearly expresses a vengeful surge in Hamlet's soul and needs no emotional overlay to make its point. When Gertrude says: "Thou turn'st mine eyes into my very soul/And there I see such black and grained spots/As will not leave their tinct.", the words so perfectly encapsulate her guilt that to paint 'guilt' on top of them is redundant. Of course speeches need to be tinted with the emotion they are expressing, but not submerged; otherwise the feeling diffuses the words and one gets neither the emotion nor the poetry. — What happens in a lot of bad American productions is that the audience is asked to accept a banal emotional reaction in place of the subtlety-of-feelings expressed in the text. And to assume that the veracity of an emotion is somehow superior to the language which poetically contains it is to misunderstand entirely the nature of blank verse and the conventions in which Shakespeare wrote.

Which bring us to what is probably the major stumbling block in American Shakespearean acting.

It is generally acknowledged even by proponents of The Method, which is essentially a bastardization of Stanislavsky's original System, that although highly effective with contemporary plays, it seems to fail miserably with classics. Why is that?

A classic is more than the sum total of its characters and situations. It inhabits a time-frame which conditions both the thoughts and speech of its characters. It's contained in a philosophic framework, different from our own which, in most instances, can bridge the past with the present but nevertheless, never loses its original stylistic character. To bring it from its own time-frame into our own, an imaginative leap is required on the part of actors and directors. Like vintage wine being poured from old bottles into new, the process needs delicate handling so that the transfer from one vessel to the other will be successful. The key to all of these transfers is an understanding of the work's original style, so that in modifying, altering or even departing from that style, we're still dealing with the ideological content which gave the original work its value.

The Method's style is, as it were, built-in. Its DNA spawned by Stanislavsky and then co-opted by Strasberg, has inescapable characteristics — just as biological DNA has basic and inescapable genetic components. It seeks to strike a balance between the actor's sense of reality and the characters', no matter what period-differences may exist. The actor translates his character's thoughts and emotions through his own, the assumption always being that human nature is constant and what was essentially true for one century remains the same for succeeding generations.

But of course, history shows us that is not the case. That, for example, there were certain class-distinctions in earlier centuries which no longer apply today and so the resultant behavior has to be either modified or altered. We know that in the 17th century, people's ideas about religion and their relation to the deity were different from our own; that a belief-system like the Chain of Being, for instance, can't possibly apply to a contemporary sensibility where atheism, agnosticism and even heresy are legitimate modes of thought.

Knowing these things and trying to make sense of them in a modern context involves very delicate adaptations to the language and behavioral-life of another time. It's not a matter of pulling a switch from Period to Modern, but of evolving a contemporary style which will permit the original style to be refashioned without violating those elements which made it worth preserving in the first place. A style goes in search of a style; a text looks for connotations and inferences which, acknowledging its original meaning, will make it meaningful again in our own time.

Because The Method's style is, as I say, built-in and because it encourages the personal styles of the actors employing it to suffuse the work, the whole question of stylistic integrity is virtually ignored. Like a steamroller, The Method flattens the classic and then tacitly demands that it rises up and become as vertical as it was before. If the classic is written in blank verse, The Method actor, imposing the rhythms that seem truest to his nature — rather than *its* nature — assumes it will assimilate whatever rhythm he chooses to give it. Poetry gets prosified, historicity is contemporized. Because he divines certain social insights which, in his mind, give it contemporary relevance, he forces it out of its doublet and hose and into jeans and t-shirts. The assumption is always the same: I can make sense of this old work by trickling it through the sieve of my modern sensibility. I *understand* Hamlet's vacillation (I too have found it hard to make up my mind about returning to school or getting a job), Macbeth's ambition (I once wanted to be manager of a company and schemed to get rid of a rival), Othello's jealousy (I once thought this bitch was two-timing me and went slightly off my rocker), Angelo's duplicity (I once wanted this girl to sleep with me in return for getting her brother a cushy job with the firm).

In a thousand minuscule different ways, the grandeur and size of Shakespeare's characters are whittled down to what Method actors conceive as viable parallels, and then played in such a way as to utterly obliterate their intrinsic meaning. In the trade-off (in which the classic is consistently shortchanged), the actor substitutes behaviorism for elegance, contemporary speech-patterns for literary constructs and verisimilitude for period style.

All of this poisoned fruit drops off the branches of the Learning Tree. Exceptional actors always manage to burst the bonds of banal and routinized training, those musty and atrophied precepts and mechanical exercises which are listlessly repeated from one semester to the next. They manage to survive the cloying effects of what we deludedly celebrate as American Education, and distinguish themselves in the profession. The fault, dear Brutus, is not in our 'stars' — but in our rank-and-file subjected to the wooly-minded, Method-bound, training programs throughout the length and breadth of America which perpetuate the mediocrity we regularly find on our metropolitan and regional stages. Instead of excavating for new means and coming up with new solutions, these instructors simply rehash, routinize, or sit back and rest on their tenures while their graduates perpetuate moribund traditions.

* * *

One can never 'sum-up' a subject as diverse as Shakespearean acting and I may have complicated the issue by ranging into questions of Elizabethan history, acting-technique, and interpretation. So rather than 'sum up; I will simply wrap up.

Clearly a naturalistic/behaviourist approach to Shakespeare goes against something in the very grain of blank verse, and a meticulous observance of prosody — by itself — isn't enough to animate the endless interpretational possibilities in the canon.

I don't know that anyone can devise an ideal formula for playing Shakespeare, but if such a panacea is ever found, paradoxically it will exemplify fastidious attention to original verse-structure and fresh insights into the social, psychological and metaphysical layers that keep the plays from becoming dead relics.

The poetic answer to this puzzle may be: — actors and directors that try to reanimate these plays must contain within themselves a perceptiveness and originality that are themselves 'Shakespearean', and strike a balance between invention and preservation just as Shakespeare himself created an equilibrium between formal structures and freewheeling experimentation.

And we the public must persistently reject reductiveness, mindless orthodoxy and arbitrary novelty just as we must embrace healthy innovation, unexpected *rev*elation and the ever-present possibility that the oldest and most familiar art can still astonish and revive even the most jaded sensibilities.

RETROFITTING CORIOLANUS

Marowitz

BYRON JENNINGS *as the title character in The Globe Theatres' 1988 production of* CORIOLANUS, *by William Shakespeare, directed by John Hirsch.* Photo by Will Gullette.

Shortly after the Irangate hearings in Washington and immediately before the presidential election of 1988, the Old Globe Theatre in San Diego presented a modern-dress production of CORIOLANUS in an adaptation by John Hirsch. In many ways, this was a typically American exercise in Shakespearean revisionism the likes of which one might encounter in Stratford, Connecticut, the New York Shakespeare Festival or, for that matter, England's National Theatre. This was Shakespeare up-dated, transplanted geographically (from Rome to Washington DC and Nicaragua), the text interpolated with colloquial additions and the whole posture altered so as to be contemporaneous with recent events. In short, the kind of production that causes seizures among the purists and transports of delight among those who like their classics liberally spiced up.

Being an intelligent and well-directed production (John Hirsch was also the director), it struck me as a useful test-case for the jazzification of Shakespeare which, more and more, takes place on American and European stages, and I am considering it here — not so much for its own sake — but as an example of what happens when the parameters of Shakespeare's works are extended (some would contend, contracted) to accommodate fresh ideas.

The play's central character, no longer a Roman warrior but now a be-medalled Marine officer redolent of Oliver North, is seen triumphant in battles against a (presumably) Central American force resembling the Sandanistas. Back from the wars, Coriolanus is feted at the Capitol and primed for a position of supreme leadership, the Senate and the political Establishment clearly bent on exploiting his military victory for the furtherance of their own national aims. Volumnia, the war-hero's mother, here consigned to a wheelchair, is a kind of crippled Washington matriarch; Virgilia, a doting, suburban wife who, Jackie Kennedy-like, clasps her tiny children to her and lends conspicuous support to her celebrated warrior-husband at all public occasions. Coriolanus himself, suffused with his traditional pride, is a surly tool of the state of which he is nevertheless, an integral part.

For the first five minutes of the performance, you find yourself recoiling from the slack diction, the prosaic interpolations and the gratuitous switch of period but, as the evening progresses, the consistency of Hirsch's vision and a highly-disciplined mise-en-scene persuades us that this is as legitimate an approach as any other. And even as some part of our higher intellect registers objections to the portrayal of Menenius Agrippa as a kind of wily Huey Long with a Southern drawl and Coriolanus as a Gung-Ho, super-patriot, the conviction behind the acting and the audacity behind the conception gradually win us over.

There is no disputing the fact that the verse was gabbled and the nuances of Shakespeare's text became the first casualties of Hirsch's guerrilla-tactics against the play but then, if one exchanges Plutarch for the Pentagon and swords for sub-machine guns, there is a kind of logic in prosifying, even coarsening, Shakespeare's strict verse patterns. The verbal interpolations (colloquial military epithets mixed with low-brow slang) sounded like gross actor-improvs (which is probably what they were) and clashed harshly with what we heard and comprehended of the original, but it was often a salutary clash producing a novel, theatrical frisson in the midst of a play which, approached in too august terms, often delivers considerably less than its author's grand design.

Hirsch used a bank of video monitors as a kind of Greek chorus to comment on the transplanted Roman action and there were regular news-updates describing the progress of the war as well as commercials promoting Coriolanus' victories. We began to experience the action through the medium of the media — the way we do most modern guerrilla wars.

At first, it was as if the performance were a pungent news program superimposed over a classical selection from a BBC Prom concert and ultimately, with the insistent static of two stations competing for the same air-wave, the listener had to opt for one or the other. For those who opted for Shakespeare Pure, this CORIOLANUS appeared as nothing more than a noisome intrusion, a travesty of the original, but for those prepared to accept Hirsch's harsh metaphors and transplanted settings, the play came through with a new kind of clarity and excitement — derived directly from the switch into a more immediate, more recognizable social framework.

As the evening progressed, one became aware that the parallels simply did not jibe. Coriolanus suffers from hubris and is an unapproachable patrician who despises the mob. Oliver North suffers from misguided chauvinism, is the darling of the plebs and, had he wanted to, could have knocked George Bush off the Republican ticket in '88 and written his own. The tension between Coriolanus and Aufidius, here dramatized as a rivalry between an American military commander and a Central American guerilla-chieftain, had no immediate contemporary parallel. North was not an active combatant, but an inside facilitator for right-wing American power-blocs. North's nemesis wasn't really the Sandanistas, it was the United States congress to whom he lied out of a corrupted sense of anti-Communist fervor. There is no character in Shakespeare's play who can 'stand in' for President Ronald Reagan, for whom North was a 'patriot' and at whose behest he committed acts which caused him to run afoul of the law. The pieces of the 'conception' and the political events on which they are based refused to marry up. However, during the course of the evening, the contemporary events were replaced by those in Shakespeare's play and, despite jolting contradictions here and there, we came to accept the Marine hero, the senators and the politicians merely as surrogates for the play's original characters. That is, we came to experience Shakespeare's play through the glass proffered by the director/adapter and, consciously or unconsciously, made allowances for the discrepancies — as, I would imagine, allowances were made for Orson Welles' fascist-dress version of JULIUS CAESAR in the thirties where again, the 'parallels' did not exactly fit but were close enough for one story to inform the other.

At the end of the performance, there was an odd kind of blur between the play and the play-imposed-upon-the-play. We had an experience which was part-Shakespearean and part-documentary. We were told a story of a patrician Roman general who ran afoul of a populace which would have liked to embrace him and another story, about a soldier who, reprimanded for his conduct in battle, refused to accept the egregious connotations placed upon it. We were given, in unequal portions, a wodge of Roman history and a slice of political current events. We were in Rome and in Washington. In Antium and Nicaragua. In a theatre and in a television-studio. In the past and in the present.

The highly stylized battle-scene from the 90-minute collage "CAESAR", *adapted and directed by Marowitz and premiered at the Humboldt Arts Festival in Northern California.*
Photograher Unknown.

What, ultimately, were the advantages of Hirsch's imposition upon Shakespeare's CORIOLANUS?

He 'translated' Shakespeare's Roman events into recent political events which, because of their notoriety and political impact, added another dimension to the given material. This new 'dimension' contained a number of attitudes and feelings to the play without which we would have had to rely on traditional and historical reconstructions. The production's aggressive modernism brought with it a whole slew of emotions which, strictly speaking, do not belong to CORIOLANUS but which nevertheless, augment the original story and secrete potent dramatic overtones. Many Americans felt strongly about Oliver North; about Reagan's frustrated attempts to aid the contras; about the political implications of intercession in Central America. Irrelevant as all these 'feelings' might be to Shakespeare's original design, they were activated by Hirsch's scenario and mingled with that other set of emotions generated by the original Roman subject. Two sets of feelings began to work simultaneously — those generated by Shakespeare's story and those superimposed by the contemporary parallels.

One could argue that one set of feelings canceled out the other, and that the price Hirsch paid for introducing arbitrary elements was to weaken and divert the stronger ones already contained in Shakespeare's play. Having created a paradigm composed of Nicaragua, the Pentagon and Oliver North, there is some part of the audience's psychology which expects a pay-off to these new narrative strands, and since the original play effectively dismantled them as it went along, there was a cumulative sense of frustration. Towards the end, if we were engrossed at all, it was in Shakespearean considerations: will Volumnia be able to persuade Coriolanus to forsake the Volscians and avoid the ruin of Rome? How will Aufidius deal with Coriolanus's betrayal? Questions very far removed from the implications of Oliver North's behavior at the Senate hearings or the fate of the contras in light of the government's refusal to underwrite aid.

Ultimately one asks, what in fact *was* paralleled here? And the answer is: personality types and vague resemblances between

Roman action and recent American events! And what caused the parallels to break down? Personality-types and vague resemblances between Roman action and recent American events! But another question is begged: did the emotional accretions of the new information in any way help the telling of the original story? As much as one is inclined to say they did not — that one was at odds with the other — the palpable fact is, they did. By being able to identify Coriolanus with a contemporary figure about whom most people held strong opinions, a dimension was added to the Shakespearean experience which, in a 'classical' version of the play, would not have emerged. Weighing the value of that new dimension against the dilution of the play's original premise throws one into a quandary. It is true that a marvelously performed, traditional version of Shakespeare's CORIOLANUS might well have produced *reverberations* of recent historical events and, at the same time, maintained the integrity of the play's original intentions. But would it have been able to harness the strong feelings generated by these specific parallels? Is it not more likely that we would have lost a certain political dimension by being visually restricted to the ancient Roman milieu?

In Gunter Grass's THE PLEBIANS REHEARSE THE UPRISING, CORIOLANUS, or rather Brecht's Marxist rescension of the play, is also used as a framework for a different dramatic experience. In Brecht's rendering, Shakespeare's hero is depicted as an enemy of the working-class and his 'pride' is seen as a tragic flaw which is condemned by the social-consciousness of the plebians. "Brecht," writes Grass in his introduction "reduces his Coriolan to the level of an efficient specialist who, though useful in time of war, oversteps his functions in peacetime and is therefore dismissed by the people and its elected tribunes … Brecht's Coriolan is swept aside because he behaves like a reactionary and fails to understand the sign of the times, the springtime of the young Roman Republic."

In Grass's play, we are at two removes from Shakespeare. He has composed his play to indict Brecht himself who, during the uprising of June 1953, "did not interrupt his rehearsals" to provide support for the protesting workers soon to be mowed down by the

Soviet tanks and the East German police. Grass's concern is not so much the ambiguous nature of Shakespeare's character, but of Brecht himself — the 'poet of the masses' who at the height of the workers' rebellion in East Germany ended a letter addressed to Ulbricht, the Soviet High Commissioner in Germany and the Premier of the German Democratic Republic, with the words: "At this moment I feel the need of expressing my solidarity with the Socialist Unity Party of Germany."

Brecht's reangling of CORIOLANUS was an overt attempt to bring a modern political consciousness to bear on a play which, in its original form, sidestepped an issue that, historically speaking, could not have occurred to Shakespeare; a ploy similar to that in TRUMPETS AND DRUMS, his rewrite of Farquhar's THE RECRUITING OFFICER. In both works, Brecht, the revisionist, legitimately stakes out a classic and proceeds both to rethink and re-angle it according to his own political lights; a thoroughly legitimate activity among contemporary playwrights and directors. But in Hirsch's case, which is the case of many contemporary directors, the revisionism is imposed on the classical text in the form of external change in the hope that new implications will smother those of the original. When Brecht reorders Shakespeare or Farquhar or Marlowe for his own purposes, he is unequivocally indicating that he wishes to alter the plays' original ideology. He clearly has another ideology to put in its place and he is using the plays' received ideas as jumping-off points for new statements and implications. In so doing, he is deliberately tinkering with the original organism in order to produce another. But when directors without Brecht's intellectual gifts approach a classic and merely spray it with alien ideas in the hope that their paint job will obliterate the original, the effect is often that the new gloss merely calls attention to the color it is attempting to replace.

In Shakespearean reinterpretation, there are basically two angles of attack: the Frontal Assault or The Subversion From Within. In the case of the former, it is sometimes possible to produce a startling sense of disorientation by which two sets of antithetical ideas cohabit the same work of art. The success of that mix depends on the relevance of the new ideas to the original and, to an even greater extent, how much of the original play is revitalized by the infusion of those ideas. In the case of the Subversion From Within, the engine of the original play is actually restructured, its original ideas re-routed, to arrive at a completely new terminus — and usually, one the author never intended. The second approach almost always demands textual liberties, revisions and the incorporation of new material. But in both cases, the thematic implications of the original work are both feeding and being conditioned by the insertion of new material — which is why, ultimately, the experiment is intrinsically Shakespearean since without the stance and caste of the original play, the recension would be unthinkable.

Contrasted with these approaches, there is the practice of merely bouncing a work off the surface of the original classic — as, for instance, KISS ME KATE is bounced off of TAMING OF THE SHREW or WEST SIDE STORY off of ROMEO AND JULIET or ROSENCRANTZ AND GUILDENSTERN ARE DEAD off of HAMLET. In these instances, Shakespeare functions merely as a pretext for new works — in much the same way that Greek, Roman and medieval sources served to propel Shakespeare into works only tangentially related to his own plays. The link here is tenuous and the cultural sovereignty of the new work is largely independent of the work on which it is based — so much so that audiences can appreciate the latter with virtually no knowledge of the former.

For the past two hundred years or so, we have experienced a variety of frontal assaults on Shakespeare's works and today, we are very accustomed to the torrents of new wine being poured into the old bottles. But internal subversions of the plays are much less common and much less acceptable — perhaps because they require an ingenuity and mechanism every bit as sophisticated as the ones they appear to be replacing. In many ways, Brecht has come closest — because he accepted the authority of Shakespeare's original work and disputed the author on an equal level of discourse. Of course, for many, Brecht's partisanship dilutes the effect of his adaptations. In most cases, Shakespeare is whittled down for the sake of an arbitrary Marxist reading and no amount of clever political engineering can atone for the loss of poetic complexity. But nevertheless, in Brecht, the principle is sound. If you want the classic to mean something else, you don't merely *intone* it differently — you dig into its innards and transform its basic constituents.

The biggest, wettest and scaliest of all red herrings is the charge that this is distorting the originals. In a sense, the originals exist *in order to be* distorted. The practice of all modern art involves the twisting of traditional materials — distortion is part of the modern painter's means-of-expression — just as dissonance is part of the musician's and contrapuntal movement part of the dancer's. The real nemesis of Shakespearean reinterpretation is the crudity and banality of so many of those 'new ideas' being foisted onto the originals. Painting a mustache on the Mona Lisa is a good once-only joke, but if Duchamps had proceeded to give Little Boy Blue a pecker or Rembrandt's Self-Portrait a black-eye, we would quickly tire of the effrontery. In the case of most classical directors, a theme of crippling obviousness is grafted onto plays which are models of enthralling complexity, thereby proclaiming the intellectual paucity of the innovations. If the creation of heavyweight blank verse drama involves Herculean skills of composition, harder still is the accretion of new dramatic ideas to augment and enliven the effect of the original. And this is because, in many cases, the deeper import of Shakespeare's original plays are not clearly understood or only partially unearthed. As Jan Kott says elsewhere in this book, there are certain plays which at certain times *become* contemporary because of a confluence between recent events and past history. When, at such times, a classic stands at the crossroads, it opens up a third way for a play to go. That happened during the occupation of France in the case of Jean Anouilh's ANTIGONE. It happened again during Olivier's HENRY V in war-time England and Jean Vilar's version of UBU ROI which roundly demolished the myth of General Charles de Gaulle. It tends to happen every so often when a modern sensibility connects or counteracts with a great play of the past, and when it does, we find ourselves talking about a classic being 'revitalized'. In the future, it may more often take the form of encountering a classic with a completely new physiognomy and an entirely different kind of diction, remembering what it used to look and sound like, and appreciating the reincarnation which now stands before us.

TWO NIGHTS OF LOVE:

ROMEO, JULIET, TROILUS & CRESSIDA

Conversation between Kott and Marowitz.

Romeo has one night of love with Juliet and then tragedy ensues. Troilus spends one night with Cressida and then both their worlds fall apart. What is the correlation between those four characters and those two plays?

It's curious. You start with the characters and I begin with the situation which, in certain ways are similar or parallel in both cases, although the characters, of course, are very different. Romeo is very different from Troilus; Cressida somewhat less different from Juliet.

But what strikes me is not so much the difference between these characters but the fact that their situations are almost identical. — What are those similarities? It is the first night of sex for both Juliet and Cressida. Juliet is fourteen and Cressida fairly close to that age, about seventeen. The next morning, Pandarus is coming to take Cressida to the Greek camp in exchange for a Trojan general. As for Romeo and Juliet, they belong to two distinct classes that share a strong hatred for each other. Cressida's situation is somewhat different. The world here is, of course, divided between Greeks and Trojans and the sexual partners are caught up in this clash, and the outside world bitterly divides the lovers.

Cressida is very witty and malicious, sometimes contemptuous of others; a type rather closer to our modern, sharp-witted young girls than Juliet. She's not naive. She is living in a rather complicated society and in a wartime situation; a war that has been going on for several years. Juliet, on the other hand, is a much more domesticated creature; very much cosseted at home. Nevertheless, the outside world is impinging on all four of these characters, invading their beds, so to speak. At the crucial moment, we have Troilus and Cressda in bed and Romeo and Juliet in bed, both in a kind of large filmic close-up, as if the outside world doesn't exist. Nothing exists but themselves. Then, the following morning, the scene is radically changed. The agent of change is, of course, different: Romeo has to flee because he has killed Paris and cannot possibly remain in Verona, and in TROILUS AND CRESSIDA the agent of change is Pandarus who comes to take Cressida away to the Greek camp.

But in both cases, you're saying, objective reality intrudes into their personal lives and causes separation.

Exactly. And, as always in Shakespeare, the family strife and the Trojan War, although each is quite different, can be seen as a metaphor. Considered abstractly, on one side there's the World and on the other the Lovers and, as always, the World is hostile to the Lovers.

Do you believe, as certain critics have suggested, that Troy stands for one kind of sensibility and Greece for another? That there is some kind of intended dichotomy between Reason and Instinct, Mind and Heart? That these two locations have a metaphorical significance?

No, no, I don't. And I cannot subscribe to these simplistic distinctions between Soul and Body, Heart and Mind. For me those kinds of oppositions appear very artificial; or leastwise, not true to the Shakespearean world.

You know it was Dover Wilson who came up with that distinction; that Troy stands for one thing; Greece, for another. Do you not acknowledge any representational differences at all between these states?

Of course there are two different images at play here and for a long time in understanding this play, it seemed very important to discriminate the differences between Troy and Greece. As we know, England believes itself to be the descendant of Troy, after the legend of Aeneas. But you know, T.B. Spencer told me once that just before the outbreak of the Second World War, when Chamberlain came to Germany suing for peace, the first great production of TROILIUS AND CRESSIDA was being performed in England and the majority of young Englishmen who saw that production identified themselves with the Greeks rather than the Trojans.

But in your writings, you have suggested that in the Elizabethan era, Greece stood for Spain and Troy stood for England. Do you still believe that?

At the time of the Great Armada, it seemed to me that England, this chivalrous country with its strong emphasis on honor, might well have thought of itself more in terms of Greece, as opposed to Spain which, being the more pragmatic state, identified itself with Troy.

If that was *the case in Elizabethan times, how would they have interpreted a play like* TROILUS AND CRESSIDA*?*

I'm not sure. You'd really have to put that question to an historian. But it seems to me that these distinctions between the two states, their symbolic conception of themselves, would not have had the same connotations then as they have for us today. I think that for Elizabethans, countries like Greece and Troy or Italy and Spain would have been perceived the way we think of Illyria. What is more important for us, is simply to recognize the oppositions. Not so long ago, there was a production of this play set during the Crimean War in which the Turks were depicted as the Trojans. But it seems to me that we can unravel TROILUS AND CRESSIDA without lumbering them with precise, nationalist parallels.

Isn't that in fact, a highly pedantic way of doping out Shakespeare's plays?

True, it's in no way essential. But it may have some importance for the *production* of these plays in that one can use a sense of period, distinctive costumes and scenery, to symbolize Greece or Ilium; a visual guide to suggest two warring states.

I want to read you a short excerpt from Marilyn French about this play. — - "Women in both Troy and Greece are mere counters; objects to be bought and sold, won or traded, bragged about, fought over or demeaned according to the owners' momentary needs. TROILUS *is really about a totally male world. It ranges from the locker room, to the battlefield to the senate chamber. Women appear in it as instruments of male will. Their names advanced as causes are simply a masking shorthand, euphemisms for the men's own motivation." — How does that strike you?*

This is of course the contemporary blah-blah of feminism in which virtually all of Shakespeare's play can be read as the mirror image of the patriarchal society. But this line of reasoning could apply just as readily to almost anything written before the 20th century. It doesn't shed any real light on the discussion of plays such as ROMEO AND JULIET and TROILUS AND CRESSIDA. And one could actually put forward the opposite view because, if you look at a play like TROILUS, the character who is most witty, independent, self-confident and self-consciously aware, is Cressida. She is also, by far, the most appealing. Troilus is rather mean, not particularly courageous. He does nothing to save Cressida from her fate and never comes to her defense. And later in the play, he is just an onlooker to her shame. In virtually all of Shakespeare's plays, the female characters are almost always more appealing, and certainly more human than the males.

I think French was referring here to Helen. That Helen is just a cause for the male characters in the play, essentially a token to be fought over by both sides.

This is just more blah-blah feminism. Helen, for at least fourteen hundred years, was the archetype of female beauty; from Homer through Marlowe and Goethe, and so on. To ask why Helen is not Archimedes or Socrates is just foolish. There is also a kind of supernatural quality to her beauty; almost as if she were a goddess. And she, as we know, was the cause of the Trojan War. This is the "face that launched a thousand ships".

So you feel this should be taken as a 'given'.

Exactly.

Now bear in mind that Romeo was as unfaithful to Rosaline as Cressida was to Troilus. If TROILUS AND CRESSIDA *is largely about infidelity and disillusioned love, can* ROMEO AND JULIET *really be said to be about constancy and romantic love?*

First of all, Romeo didn't sleep with Rosaline.

No, but he was in love with her.

He was in love but didn't consummate his love and, within the context of ROMEO AND JULIET, the affair was something of an exuberant juvenile fantasy; a young boy's infatuation. And so it's quite wrong to suggest that Romeo was unfaithful to Rosaline because clearly, they had nothing in common.

Perhaps, but he seemed to be as much in love with Rosaline as he shortly would be with Juliet. He makes quite a song and dance of it to Benvolio. Didn't he, as adolescents often do, simply transfer his passion from one girl to the other?

That you would have to ask him. — Look, in the scene to which you refer, it's quite clear that Benvolio is not taking his infatuation very seriously. 'O, you'll easily find another girl. Go to the bar and compare the girls there with your Rosaline and you'll soon find one just as good.'

All right, let's accept that for the moment. Isn't the larger point here that ROMEO AND JULIET *is a romanticization of love and* TROILUS AND CRESSIDA *about the disillusionment of love.*

I don't know what you mean by 'romanticization'. 'Romantic ' is the word that the 19th century used to describe many of the works of Shakespeare.

I'll try to be more specific. In ROMEO AND JULIET, *there is a kind of idealization of love but in* TROILUS AND CRESSIDA, *a certain cynicism creeps in and sours the love between the young soldier and the girl. And whereas Juliet is depicted as an innocent young girl suffused with love, Cressida emerges almost as a kind of whore.*

I strongly disagree. In both cases, we have two very young girls, both of them virgins. If one were a director advising the young actress playing Cressida, one would not say that her character was cynical. She is *using* cynicism to defend herself. It's much more a *mask*-of-cynicism that she adopts because she is somehow afraid of love, and of sex while at the same time somewhat curious.

You're saying she uses irony strictly as a defense?

As a defense, and also as a way of camouflaging her deeper feelings. In a changed situation, Cressida could have been entirely faithful to Troilus because the betrayal here was not Cressida's against Troilus, but Troilus's against Cressida. He never came to Cressida's defense and ultimately, it was Troilus who abandoned Cressida. — Let me try to give you an example of what I'm saying here.

Once I gave an exercise to some of my students which consisted of a kind of post-mortem dialogue between Troilus and Cresssida, in the other world, long after both of them were dead. What kind of words would they speak to one another if they were to suddenly meet again in that limbo? One of the best essays that was handed in consisted of an exchange between the two ex-lovers in which Cressida says "O, Troilus I have missed you so fiercely. I have been so desperate to see you again. It has been so long." And Troilus responds: 'And who exactly are you?" "I am Cressida!" answers the spirit in surprise. "Cressida? Cressida?" says Troilus wide-eyed. "I'm sorry I don't remember any Cressida."

So in your view, Troilus was the faithless one.

Of the two, Troilus is the mean character.

Simply because he didn't come to Cressida's defense?

If, as a director, you were obliged to cast an actor to play Troilus, it would be a very different type of young man than you would choose for Romeo.

What sort of actor would you cast as Troilus?

(Pause) A Trojan playboy. — You remember at the beginning of the play when all the soldiers are going off to battle, Troilus stays behind..

Because he's in love.

Yes, he's in love and that's his justification for not going off to the battle. To my mind, he's something of a coward as a soldier just as he is something of a coward as a lover. Shakespeare is always building these oppositions into his plays. For instance the opposition between Hector and Troilus. Troilus has not been heroically designed; he hasn't the guts to be a hero. Hector, on the other hand, is the hero of all heroes.

When Cressida is given over to the Greek camp in exchange for a famous Trojan general, what could Troilus have done?

That's a good question. But it's very difficult to apply such realistic considerations in a play like this.

But if you blame Troilus for not coming to Cressida's defense, you have to come up with reasons for that charge.

But if you look to the plot — and not *outside* of the plot — when Cressida is brought to the Greek camp and confronted by the Greek leaders, she feels extremely contemptuous of Troilus. She feels betrayed. So you ask: what could Troilus do to defend Cressida in this situation? In theory, he could have done lots of things, but to suggest them would be extraneous to Shakespeare's plot. The fact is what she feels most strongly at that moment is a strong sense of betrayal. And having been betrayed by Troilus she feels justified in reacting in a spirit of revenge.

And that's why she goes with Diomedes?

It's not just that she's making herself available to Diomedes. She's also, remember, giving him Troilus' gift of the sleeve.

In giving that gift, is she not blatantly betraying Troilus?

The gift signifies that *she* has been betrayed and so is justified in using that token of love to betray her betrayer. Shakespeare is always pushing his situations to the furthest limits. Given her character, it was not obligatory for Cressida to become a whore. Ultimately, she acknowledges it herself in that brief exchange with Thersites, you remember:

Ah, poor our sex! this fault in us I find,
The error of our eye directs our mind.
What error leads must err: oh then conclude.
Minds swayed by eyes are full of turpitude.

To which Thersites replies:

A proof of strength she could not publish more
Unless she said. "My mind is now turned whore."

There's something arbitrary about the way Cressida's character changes when she's delivered to the Greeks. As soon as she arrives, everyone takes turns kissing her; she seems to be suddenly sophisticated, even saucy; suddenly very "grown up'. — Is that sudden shift of character not a fault in the playwright?

There are two or three points here. Cressida arrives at the Greek camp; she is unfaithful to Troilus; she sleeps with Diomedes, but for Shakespeare, who is always pushing circumstances to the extreme, that was not enough. For him, it was necessary that she actually becomes a whore in the Greek camp.

But that extreme change has to come out of something in the character, doesn't it?

It comes, first of all, from tradition; the legend that Cressida represents the archetype of the unfaithful woman. But it is also Shakespeare's natural tendency to push conflicts to their furthermost conclusion. He does the same in ROMEO AND JULIET with the poisoned potion. When Juliet awakes in the tomb and finds Romeo expired, that is not enough. Shakespeare finds it necessary for her to then commit suicide. Because in a divided world, to a young girl who has given both her body and soul to the boy she loved, Fate decrees that she too must die. With another kind of playwright, someone who was not Shakespeare, it would not have to be to that extreme, but for Shakespeare, depicting a divided world in which lovers belong to different and opposing sects, love has to cease and the lovers must be fatally divided.

But in TROILUS AND CRESSIDA, *there is no such tragic denouement. Cressida lives; Troilus lives.*

It's important to define here what we understand as tragedy. A tragedy is the annihilation of laughter. The fall of Cressida, or transformation of one of Shakespeare's most beautiful and appealing female characters into a whore, seems to me to fall into the category of tragedy. To my mind, TROILUS AND CRESSIDA is a much more moving tragedy than ROMEO AND JULIET. Let me give you another example.

During the war, I was occasionally asked to give lectures to members of the Polish underground. It often comprised very young boys and girls who had committed themselves to subverting the enemy, assassinating German officers, blowing up enemy transports etc. Of course, it was slightly idiotic to give lectures to a group of young people who, no sooner had they been exposed to questions of art and literature, had then to go and blow up trains or kill enemy soldiers, but it was a diversion I suppose, and so I did it.

In one of these groups, there was a very young, very beautiful, very sweet-natured girl. One night she slept, for the first time, with one of the young boys from the group and the next morning, the boy had to leave to perform one of the group's most hazardous assignments: to kill the new chief of the S.S. in Warsaw. And in executing this assignment, which was actually successful, the young boy, after his first and only night with this beautiful girl, was killed.

For many months afterward, the girl never left her bed — night nor day. She ate there, she read there, she wrote there — she was something of poetess — had many male visitors and fucked every man that came to see her in that room. Then, one night, some kind of change came over her. She left her bed and went off with members of her group to mine the railway-lines and blow up the trains transporting German soldiers to the front. She went on to become a fiercely committed resistance-fighter.

So if we refer this back to Cressida and compare her to the underground-girl, there is another set of options for someone in a similar situation. The girl from the underground became neither a whore nor a suicide but took a third course and become a militant activist.

In plays like ROMEO AND JULIET and TROILUS AND CRESSIDA, you have brief chronicles of the human condition. They suggest there are only two dramatic, tragic, cruel possibilities: suicide or rampant promiscuity. If a true, meaningful life becomes impossible, then those appear to be the only two alternatives. But it may be possible to find a third, not necessarily in drama but perhaps in real life; perhaps not so much in peace-time, but more likely during war. In cases like Cressida's, promiscuity becomes a form of contempt for love. And sometimes, instead of taking one's own life, one commits oneself to a kind of dangerous integrity which still puts one's life at risk. Either one gives one's body to a series of strangers (which is one way of sacrificing one's own life) or commits it to some idealized cause outside of oneself, which also poses a threat to one's life.

In TROILUS, *it sometime feels to me as if Shakespeare is writing tongue-in-cheek; mocking the honor and the heroism of all these grandiose characters, but I think you feel that isn't very unique.*

No, it's not very unique at all. There is a long tradition for heroics and of course, *anti*-heroics and, from about the late Middle Ages, there has always been a certain amount of mockery of heroes.

Particularly those of the Trojan War?

Especially the image of Helen as a kind of Queen of Beauty who is also something of a legendary whore.

TROILUS & CRESSIDA *seems to represent a much more disillusioned view of love than* ROMEO AND JULIET *which was written just about five or six years before. Do you feel this is Shakespeare dealing with very similar material but in a very different way?*

I agree. TROILUS AND CRESSIDA is perhaps the darkest of all the dark plays with perhaps MEASURE FOR MEASURE having the distinction of being the darkest. The disillusionment not only touches love and war but heroic values themselves Achilles, for instance, emerges as a coward killing Hector by very underhanded means.

This seems to be a play written by someone who is totally turned off by life and war and the kind of society that, while giving lip-service to moral platitudes, inherently breeds evil. It's as if all the idealism of the early HENRIES, CAESAR *and* HAMLET *has entirely dried up.*

Although I'm not an historian, I would agree. It may well be that a certain disillusionment set in after the Spanish Armada which may account for this attitude.

Ulysses' speech about 'degree' is often cited as being central to this play but, as depicted by Shakespeare, Ulysses is something of a hypocrite and there is nothing in the play that actually exemplifies the belief in order and degree. It all sounds a little like a commercial for the Chain of Being; a product that everyone wanted to believe in but which, more and more, was falling into disrepute. Is this a play that can be easily misinterpreted because the parts do not correspond to the whole?

I guess so, because when the speech you refer to is dissected by critics, they often see it as a great defense of law and order, positively stated and without irony. But if you take the play as a whole and relate it to Ulysses, who is both a cynic and a master of subterfuge, it is difficult to accept the speech at its face value.

Is it then simply an arbitrary declaration of commonly perceived values, something that Shakespeare often resorted to in his plays to reassure the groundlings and reaffirm the beliefs of the aristocracy?

For me the character who is perhaps closest to Shakespeare's own attitudes is Thersites. 'All you see is cowards and whores, cowards and whores' he seems to be saying. You remember that speech of his which ends: "Lechery, lechery; still wars and lechery; nothing else holds fashion: a burning devil take them." Thersites is right of course, and as an objective statement of reality we have to agree with Thersites — although from the moral standpoint, we must, of course, disagree.

It's curious though, isn't it that this play opens with Pandarus organizing a sexual assignation between his cousin Cressida and Troilus. It moves through betrayals and disenchantment and ends with Pandarus bemoaning his downfall as a pimp. It seems clear to me that this is a play about the disillusionment of love, the inability to meld moral precepts and human behavior, and yet surrounding this dark morality fable is this panoply of the Trojan War and its legendary cast of characters. I don't see how the love story ties up with the epic war story that surrounds it. Do you?

I can't say. TROILUS AND CRESSIDA has been very rarely successful on the stage and one of the mistakes that directors often make is to place the emphasis on the war and the opposing camps and not on the sexual threads that weave through this play. If the central framework is the Trojan War, it has a very different effect and a very different meaning.

But what is that meaning? Usually in Shakespeare the sub-plots and the main action are thematically linked — as in MEASURE, *for instance, there's a clear-cut symbiosis between the bordello world and Angelo's lust for Isabella, etc. but in* TROILUS, *I don't see the linkage between the story of the war and the story of the lovers.*

This seems to me quite clear. Let me put it this way. You could easily visualize a different kind of ending for TROILUS AND CRESSIDA which is that Cressida dies by her own hand or is killed by Troilus and then, to have the full tragic impact, Troilus takes his own life.

There's certainly enough motivation for such a conclusion.

Yes, but then the question is: would this be more tragic than the un-tragic ending that now exists. To my mind, such an ending would be pure pathos, unrealistic and not savoring of the cruel truth actually embedded in the play as Shakespeare wrote it. The cruelty of the play is somehow rooted in, depends upon, Troilus' cowardice and Cressida's becoming a whore.

You have to be very careful when you talk about Troilus' cowardice. Although you may call him a coward in not coming to Cressida's defense, he is very courageous at the end of the play, going off to do battle against Diomedes, to recapture his sleeve, and restore his honor.

I agree, I agree; but somehow, I cannot muster much sympathy for Troilus.

Certain critics of this play have said that it's about the impossibility of living up to high ideals or the tendency of Instinct to get the upper hand over Reason. Do you think that this is something Shakespeare was dealing with here? I know this is another one of those questions that drives you mad — i.e. 'what's going on in Shakespeare's mind' etc, — but I will ask it anyway?

It's not very easy for me either to agree or strongly disagree with what you've suggested. But when you use words like 'Instinct' or 'Reason', I don't believe these words had the same meanings for Shakespeare as they do for us today. For myself, I ask the question: what is it that happened to all the parties involved during this war, and the answer has little to do with either Instinct or Reason.

I know you shy away from talking about character, but at the beginning of this play Cressida seems to be very virtuous and in her first scene with Troilus, almost modest.

The beauty of Cressida is that she speaks very freely — very much like a contemporary French or American young lady; free from mental taboos. But then very shortly, she transforms into a very shy girl, anxiously waiting for her lover, sexually inexperienced, talking in a rather superficial way; suddenly very different from what she was when we first met her.

But in their second scene, when Cressida becomes more open, bolder, and more sexually sophisticated, is Shakespeare suggesting that we have to reconsider that modest veneer and recognize that her modesty was simply a pose that concealed a much more wily personality?

Let's imagine Cressida as she might be in real life: a seventeen year old girl, a virgin, someone who has been exposed to a multitude of experiences during the war; innocent in her body, but in her mind — her vision — her imagination — completely infested by the cruelty of war and the subterfuges of court life. As you see, what I am doing here is seeing how the situation is interpreted through the character — not assuming the character has been superimposed onto the situation. Take a typical 16 or 17 year old girl in World War II — exposed to all the normal experiences of such a time — the murders, the heroism, the cowardice, the lust, the rape and yet, she's a virgin and somehow infatuated with a young man. To simultaneously experience this attraction and repulsion as part of her first sexual experience, it's quite normal.

So you would contend the way to look at these things is from the social context first and then to divine character from that.

Because I believe that, not only as an interpretation of drama but also in terms of human behavior, all of us are the products of our social conditioning — not that our social consequences are in some way directed or resolved by our character. Our individual situations are constantly changing, of course, but it seems to me that in some way, we are all very similar.

There was a beautiful French film some years back — "The Rules of the Game" by Jean Renoir — about the French occupation, and the meaning behind this film was that during the war — during the occupation, it was the social context of our lives that turned us either into heroes or cowards. You leave your house and turn left, you are a hero. You turn right, and you're a coward.

But if you push this idea to its logical conclusion doesn't it simply lead you into fatalism?

The meaning of fatalism is that everything is in some way preordained. Everything is blocked out. Our lives are *fated.* But I'm not saying this. What I am saying is that in the complexities of life, changing from one moment to the other, especially during times of great tension like war or revolution, we are much more subject to our situation — that is, to the forces of the external world — than we are in normal circumstances. Here in America, we are usually doing what we feel we have to do. Things are fairly predictable — not unexpected. But during war-time when situations change from one hour to the next, we are much more at the mercy of outside pressures. Victims of circumstance.

In a general sense, that is true but if you take, for example, the character of Macbeth. Wouldn't you say this is an instance in which character does in fact influence social circumstance? Macbeth's character, and to a much larger extent Lady Macbeth's character, produce a drastic change in their social situation simply because of the nature of those two people. No?

Yes and no. You could start by looking at Macbeth and Lady Macbeth and conclude that everything that happens stems from their given characters. But we see quite clearly that after the murder of Duncan, Macbeth believes that is the end of the matter. He has gained the crown. He is home free. But then, the first murder necessitates another murder, and then yet another murder. Once he has destroyed the legitimate king, his situation obliges him to continue killing until he himself is killed. What occurs is completely independent of his character. The witches' prophecy, the ambitions of his wife, the fears of Banquo's succession — all these objective elements in his situation force him into the actions he performs. It's an example of what I have described previously as The Great Mechanism.

'Character is action, action character' — whatever! Here we must agree to disagree. But I would like to get back to TROILUS AND CRESSIDA *and ask you one last question about this intriguing play.*

The action of the play is inextricable from the Trojan War. It is the milieu in which everything takes place. In ROMEO AND JULIET, *everything occurs within the framework of the hostility generated by the fueding Montagues and Capulets and yet in both plays, Shakespeare is essentially exploring private issues between these respective sets of lovers. For me,* TROILUS *is almost the sub-text of* ROMEO AND JULIET *dealing with issues in a darker and more sensual way than they are treat-*

ed in the earlier play. My question is this: Do you believe that TROILUS AND CRESSIDA *could be a reworking of those themes which first appeared in* ROMEO AND JULIET *as it is alleged by some that* KING LEAR *is a reworking of* TIMON OF ATHENS. *We know that Chekhov, for instance, used* THE WOOD DEMON *almost as an ur-text for what eventually became* UNCLE VANYA. *Is this something that Shakespeare might have done — to revisit material he had treated years before in order to convey the playwright's changed attitudes to the subject matter?*

Perhaps a better example is the reworking of the ROMEO AND JULIET plot within the framework of 'Pyramus and Thisbe' in MIDSUMMER NIGHT'S DREAM No one is absolutely certain which of these plays came first. Their speculative dates of composition are almost identical — that's to say between 1594 and 1596. It looks as if the grotesque version followed the pathetic version; that's to say that THE DREAM followed ROMEO AND JULIET, but no one is sure. It's basically the very same story. Pyramus kills himself because he believes Thisbe was devoured by the lion. Another fatal mistake, and we have the joint suicide of both lovers in a rather grotesque fashion. Shakespeare, like many of great playwrights, seemed to be obsessed by the same themes and was constantly dealing with his obsessions, in one form or another.

But in regard to TROILUS, *do you think Shakespeare was consciously reworking the material of* ROMEO AND JULIET *in order to express a more cynical conclusion?*

I wouldn't necessarily use the word 'reworking' but as I've said, I think that many great artists are, constantly hallucinated, so to speak, by the same themes.

But the 'hallucination' in regard to the later play comes up with such a different texture. I feel that the author of ROMEO AND JULIET *still has a belief in the goodness of life, the possibility of redemption, but I don't feel that about the author of* TROILUS AND CRESSIDA.

You're right — because what is the end of ROMEO AND JULIET? The tragedy of the two lovers' death, and what does it produce? Reconciliation between the Capulets and the Montagues. It is, despite all the gloom and the horror, a happy ending — tragic for the lovers but happy for Verona.

And TROILUS AND CRESSIDA?

Is, in a sense, a tragi-comedy. Illusions are burst, loyalties betrayed, but the lovers live on.

And the war goes *on.*

Of course, the war goes on, and so as far as the world is concerned, there is no happy ending. It's ends on a note of pessimism. If one were to speculate about Cressida: she could go on to be a very successful Greek courtesan, maturing eventually into a rich madame of a very prosperous bordello, and Troilus might become a highly decorated general. Both of them settling into a very contented old age.

I know you resist interpreting these plays in terms of character, but isn't this a turning point in Shakespeare's own life? From here on out, through the last decade of his life, he's turning out heavy, somber and, to my mind, bitter tragedies. LEAR, TIMON, CORIOLANUS, CYMBELINE, WINTER'S TALE. *The pessimism that ends* TROILUS *seems to me to flow through all the remaining works of the canon. Is* TROILUS AND CRESSIDA *not some kind of watershed in Shakespeare's life that separates the young playwright from the older more disillusioned retiree at Stratford?*

Maybe. I don't know. I'm always somewhat loath to view Shakespeare as moving from light to dark or dark to light. It's true that the very early Shakespeare has a different kind of exuberance from the later playwright, but from MIDSUMMER NIGHT'S DREAM onward I think there is an intermingling of light and dark, and that play of sunshine and shadow remains in Shakespeare until the final fade-out.

SHAKESPEAREAN SCRAPS

Marowitz

Shakespeare, who was responsible for many 'firsts', created in Iago the first deconstructionist. Iago who "is nothing, if not critical", deconstructs Othello's relationship with Desdemona, Cassio, the rulers of Venice and, of course, himself. He does this with penetrating analyses of people's weaknesses and by skeptically questioning binary structures such as superior/inferior, true/false, love/hate, etc. In his dealings with others, he is constantly reinterpreting their language, disturbing their faultlines and playing with presuppositions and intertextualities. He understands, better than any, that image precedes ontology.

* * *

The most courageous character in the entire Canon is the Duke of Cornwall's First Servant who, after Regan has urged her husband to blind Gloucester in one eye and then finish the job by gouging out the other, suddenly intercedes to save the old man.

FIRST SERVANT: Hold your hand, my lord!
I have served you ever since I was a child;
But better service have I never done you
Than now to bid you hold.

REGAN: How now, you dog!

FIRST SERVANT: If you did wear a beard upon your chin
I'd shake it on this quarrel.

(Cornwall draws his sword.)

What do you mean?

CORNWALL: My villain!
(He lunges at him.)

FIRST SERVANT: *(drawing his sword)*
Nay then, come on, and take the chance of anger.
(He wounds Cornwall)

REGAN: Give me thy sword. A peasant stand up thus!
(She takes a sword and runs at him behind.)

FIRST SERVANT: O, I am slain! My lord, you have one eye left
To see some mischief on him. O!

The first Servant dies but his impulsive stroke against Cornwall will soon finish off the Duke as well. — What a marvelous play it would be to depict the life of the downtrodden but loyal peasant-servant of Cornwall who, after many years of suppressing repulsion at his master's cruelty, stands up to him to save Gloucester's remaining eye and then perishes in the attempt. The climactic scene of such a play would, of course, be Shakespeare's KING LEAR Act Three, Scene 7 as noted above.

* * *

If Shakespeare has one overriding fault it is that he writes too well. Every lowly, minor character receives the gift of his percipience and philosophical insight. The weave of every play is made up of the rich threads of his own wisdom and articulateness and, as a result, these characters do not so much come alive as draw literary sustenance from the man who has conceived them.

In TROILUS AND CRESSIDA for instance, after Achilles has been snubbed by the Greek high command, belittled by Ulysses and made to feel inferior because of Ajax's rising prominence, his murky, mealy-mouthed lover Patroclus, stung by these criticisms of the former hero, breaks out with:

> "A woman impudent and mannish grown
> Is not more loathed than an effeminate man
> In time of action. I stand condemned for this.
> They think my little stomach to the war
> And your great love to me restrains you thus.
> Sweet, rouse yourself, and the weak wanton Cupid
> Shall from your neck unloose his amorous fold,
> And like a dewdrop from the lion's mane,
> Be shook to air. .....

And later:

> "Those wounds heal ill that men do give themselves.
> Omission to do what is necessary
> Seals a commission to a blank of danger;
> And danger like an ague, subtly taints
> Even when they sit idly in the sun."

All of which are telling and perceptive comments but entirely out of character in Achilles' previously non-descript doxy. Almost every character in TROILUS AND CRESSIDA is made the purveyor of perspicacity and eloquence which turn them into ramifications of that omniscient intelligence which belongs to their author.

Thersites and Pandarus are not exactly interchangeable; the former possesses a satirical edge and narkyness that the latter lacks — but they share a certain crudity and salaciousness and there is a striking resemblance in the lilt of both their language. In the great disputatious scene (Act II, scene 2) in which the Trojan leaders debate whether or not to return Helen to Greece, although Priam, Hector, Troilus, Paris and Helenus express different viewpoints, the discourse is circumscribed by an all-embracing polemical diction; a common tone-of-voice — that of their creator. Today, we associate good dramatic writing with an author that defines the uniqueness of each of his several characters. In this regard, Jonson is superior to Shakespeare and even Webster has the edge on him.

Was it because of this, I wonder, that certain critics came to the conclusion that we should consider the works not so much as disparate plays but 'poems' in which theme, character and action, were all variations within one great ream of poetic text? If we were considering the weaknesses of a contemporary playwright, we would complain that an audience is overly conscious of the author's tone-of-voice and that there is no effective discrimination between one character and the next. But in Shakespeare's case, we are so carried away by the surge of the intellect and the crackle of the language, we raise no objections. We laud Shakespeare for what, in any other writer, would be a grievous fault.

*   *   *

In his own day, Shakespeare was praised as much for hi s comedies as his tragedies. In the 16th century, Francis Meres compared his comedy-writing to that of Plautus which was high praise indeed. But just as the books of many successful musical comedies from the 20s and 30s hardly raise a smile today, so much of Shakespeare's buffoonery and wordplay sound desperately forced to the modern ear. The comic situations (e.g. Malvolio ingratiating himself before Olivia because of Sir Toby's forged letter, an enamored Rosalind coercing Orlando to woo her, etc) still amuse, but much of the punning and point-scoring of the allegedly comic exchanges (Beatrice and Benedict, Petruchio and Kate, Jacques and Touchstone) come across like ancient galliards in a dance-hall given over to rap and rock'n'roll. Without a copy of Onions' 'Shakespeare Glossary' or in-depth scholarly research, much of this drollery is incomprehensible and, as Jan Kott explains elsewhere in this volume, you can't "play footnotes"

In many instances, the success of such scenes depend on the invention of comic business by imaginative actors or directors. Through mime, clever staging and farcical embellishments, almost any stale piece of material can be made to yield some ribaldry. But not to acknowledge the staleness of much of Shakespeare's comedy is simply shutting one's eye to the obvious.

Does acknowledging this diminish Shakespeare's greatness? Not a whit. But what it suggests to me is that the strength of the canon lies less in its text than in its plot-structure and charactero-logical-base. It is also, in my mind, a license to freely refurbish and plaster over the dry rot that occasionally mars the original construction.

*   *   *

The difference between John Gielgud and Laurence Olivier was the difference between gaslight and electricity. Gielgud burnt with a low, hard, constant flame that rose or descended with the flick of a switch; Olivier crackled and was incandescent. The contemplative heroes: Hamlet, Brutus, Henry VI, Richard II could have been written by Shakespeare with Gielgud in mind. The more eruptive personalities: Othello, Titus, Mercutio, Richard III, naturally receive the high voltage of Olivier's talents.

Gielgud's Hamlet, according to Robert Speaght's report was "spontaneous and unmannered...meditative but not mooning; lucid but not explanatory; active with a feverish, misdirected energy; swift and subtle without making complexity more complicated; discovering its effect in the lines and not in the business." Olivier's prince judging from the film was brooding, inchoate, suppressive and volatile. He throbbed with the kind of danger that one senses from a person who is holding an enormous amount of fury in check which might explode at any moment. But with Olivier, every wild harangue segued into a sullen reflection like a fire that sends out a great spurt of flame and then settles back to a quiet flickering. The root of Olivier's Hamlet was a palpitating sadness. One feels with Gielgud, it was probably a finely rationalized despair; a tortured man trying to make sense out of what was happening to him.

Tyrone Guthrie, who knew both actors well, put it this way; "Gielgud, although the range of his acting is smaller than Olivier's, is the more sophisticated rhetorician. When he is suited by the material, he speaks with a matchless musicality ... Oliver has developed, as he expresses it himself, the brass of his orchestra but never mastered the strings. That is to say, he commands marvelous tones for violent, exciting vocal crises and challenges, but the soft, tender luscious tones are considerably less marvelous; or, to put it technically, nasal resonance has been cultivated at the expense of the deeper, softer, resonances of chest and throat."

Another observer put it this way: "John is claret; Larry is burgundy — to which it may be added that when either is at its best, there is nothing to choose between them."

That however, is a clever oversimplification. There was quite a lot to choose between them. If you wanted a nuanced delivery of Shakespearean sense, Gielgud was the man to give it to you. He animated the text and followed every little groove and crevice in the verse. If you wanted to be swept away by unpredictable character-choices and oceanic sympathy for the character being portrayed, you turned to Olivier. In the fashions that dominated classical acting from the middle to the end of the twentieth century, Olivier seemed the more modern actor. His angst spoke to the time in stronger accents than Gielgud's languor. But he could never have played Richard II or touched the petals of the boutonniere that embroidered Gielgud's performance of John Worthing.

* * *

At the end of every comedy, Shakespeare completes the symmetry on which the plays are founded. Conflicts are resolved, misunderstandings clarified, identities reaffirmed, injustices remedied. Although we usually think of catharsis in terms of tragedy, the sense of being healthily purged applies much more to the comedies. The tragedies on the other hand, though they invariably end on a positive note, never really banish the violence and misery that has gone before. They often appear like a big red ribbon wrapped around a black-draped coffin which in no way mitigates the preceding gloom. What is curious is that Shakespeare always felt the need to point to a better future even when all the evidence he had so persuasively presented made such a prospect inconceivable.

* * *

Jews despise Shylock and abominate "The Merchant of Venice" but blacks have no such animus against Othello. In fact, despite his treachery, his violent temperament, his proclivity towards paranoia and murder, they admire him intensely. I know many Jewish actors who have declined to play Shylock, but every black actor I've ever met has wanted to play Othello.

* * *

FORD RAINEY *as the Ghost (foreground)*, FRANKLYN SEALES *(with raised sword) as* HAMLET *in the Play Scene from* THE MAROWITZ HAMLET *produced at the L.A. Theatre Centre in the the mid-70s.*
Photographer Unknown.

No amount of scholarship or historical evidence will ever convince me that Shakespeare is the author of "Pericles". It's like suggesting that Hemingway, taking a break from "The Sun Also Rises" and "Farewell To Arms", knocked off a few episodes of "The Perils of Pauline".

* * *

I despise Hamlet.

He is a slob.

A talker, an analyser, a rationalizer.

Like the parlor liberal or paralyzed intellectual, he can describe every facet of a problem, yet never pull his finger out.

Is Hamlet a coward, as he himself suggests, or simply a poseur, a frustrated actor who *plays* the scholar, the courtier and the soldier as an actor (a very bad actor) assumes a variety of roles to which he is not naturally suited.

And why does he keep saying everything twice?

And how can someone talk so pretty in such a rotten country given the sort of work he's got cut out for himself?

You may think he's a sensitive, well-spoken and erudite fellow, but frankly, he gives me a pain in the ass.

* * *

Whenever I hear that a director is going to "do Shakespeare straight" "without frills" and "in strict accordance with the text", I know I will shortly fall into a comatose state.

* * *

"The Merry Wives of Windsor" proves conclusively that when a playwright is given a commission rather than being allowed to follow his own bent, even as great an artist as Shakespeare can produce drivel. Confronted with a piece of prefabricated claptrap such as "Merry Wives", it is almost incumbent upon a director to use the material as a springboard into an original and unrelated work of art. The best "Merry Wives" I've ever seen have always been those that thoroughly deracinated the original. The worst, those that foolishly believed there was some inviolable connection between Falstaff and the Henries that spawned him.

* * *

When I asked the pupil who claimed to have an irrepressible zeal for the Bard what her two favorite Shakespearean plays were, she answered: "Romeo and Juliet."

* * *

The ideal production of THE COMEDY OF ERRORS would be played by a cast which included Bert Lahr, Milton Berle, Phil Silvers, Jimmy Durante, Eddie Cantor, Leon Errol, Martha Raye, Cass Daley, Fannie Brice, Margaret Dumont, Willie Howard, Joe Penner, Ed Wynn, W.C. Fields, Webber and Fields, Olsen and Johnson, Abbott and Costello and the Marx Brothers. Abandoning all pretense at verse-playing and consistent characterization, it would take place on a vaudeville stage with a runway down the front and incorporate every pun, sight-gag and comic shtick developed over half a century on the Klaw & Erlanger circuit. The play is Shakespeare's equivalent of Moliere's "Doctor In Spite of Himself" which is also an extended blackout-sketch and clamors to be played in that low comic style which, when essayed by outsize comedians, often rakes in the highest rewards. Plodding realistically through the minutiae of all those mistaken identity shenanigans is a bardolotrous waste of time. Shakespeare knew a good vaudeville show when he saw one but we, alas, almost never get to see the show that Shakespeare conceived.

* * *

Open Letter to Horatio:

Dear Horatio:

I know the world esteems you a 'good friend', but in my opinion you are a rotter. A good friend doesn't let *his* good friend continually delude himself. A good friend says: you've got everything going for you and if you kill the king and wrest control, everyone will support you, but if you continue to indulge in amateur theatricals and walk around with your head up your ass, you will lose what small dignity you still possess.

You are the most obnoxious Yes-man in the Shakespearean canon. I suspect that, at base, you are a careerist. If your loquacious aristocratic schoolmate ever gains control of Denmark, your future is assured. (No doubt, you have your eye on the Ministry of Education.) It isn't until the play's final moments that you realize you have been backing the wrong horse, and I wonder to what extent your passionate wails for the dying prince are a grandstand play for the new ruler. I loathe your muttering obsequiousness, your "Aye, my lord" and "No, my lord" and "Is't possible, my lord?"

It is no wonder Hamlet thinks so highly of you. You possess the very same fault that cripples him: the inability to permit conviction to give birth to action. You lack the moral gumption that makes a man forsake fruitless intellectual roundabouting for the sharp, straight path of direct action. To say that your "blood and judgement are so well commingled that they are not a pipe for Fortune's finger to sound what stop she please" is only another way of saying there is no impulse no matter how demanding that you would not be able to rationalize its reversal or abandonment. Not being "Passion's slave" is one thing, but being so devoid of passion that every rapier-thrust is converted to a pinprick is just elaborate hypocrisy. It is a fancy way of saying the mind is so much the master of the heart that nothing can be truly felt that is not first fully understood, and since honor is more a matter of the heart than the mind, this is just an excuse for evasion and cowardice.

Lord Hamlet loves you for those very qualities which prove his undoing. Like you, he is "one that suffers all yet suffers nothing" – since sufferance that doesn't lead to remedy *is* suffering nothing. Like you, "he takes Fortune's buffets and rewards with equal thanks." Fortune deprives him of a kingdom; he makes no move to recover it. Fortune has besmirched the memory of his father and, amidst much breast-beating and verbosity, he accepts the new dispensation. Fortune sends him to England; he goes. Fortune wafts him back; he returns. Fortune has him killed in a duel, and he 'defies augury' by walking straight into the trap.

If the old adage is true and one can read people by looking at their friends, then you are an accurate gauge of Hamlet's inadequacies. I have excised you from my adaptation of HAMLET since you simply hang around like an insufferable feed, wasting pedantry on soldiers who couldn't give a damn, and making false bravura gestures like drinking from a poisoned goblet that's already been emptied. I hope you will not take this personally, but the fact is that until further notice, your services will no longer be required.

* * *

One of Jacob Adler's greatest successes on the Yiddish stage was "The Yiddish King Lear", a Russian-Hebrew version of Shakespeare's family melodrama. An arrogant father cruelly betrayed by his finagling daughters, two of which bring him no-goodnick sons-in-law and the third who refuses to display that show of affection which all Jewish fathers jealously demand of their youngest. The great *macher*, after immense affluence, is reduced (in Adler's version) to a quavering blind beggar. — You can call this a despicable piece of 'shund' but, as with so many extrapolations from the canon, the centrifugal soap-opera plot is to be found smack-dab in the middle of Shakespeare's epic tragedy. — Filial ingratitude, domestic squabbles, scheming in-laws, smart-ass schlemiels offering their masters pithy advice, *altah cocker* seniors having their eyes gouged out, majesty to penury, riches to rags: how could any Jewish audience resist it?

* * *

What we look for in Shakespeare is Order; whatever the dissonances, we expect them to end in harmony. We collude with Shakespeare in believing that, conflicts and crises notwithstanding, God is in His heaven and all's right with the world. But if this is what we actually got, Shakespeare would be as negligible as Sir Richard Steele, George Lillo or any of the other sentimentalists of the late 18th century. No, what creates our kinship with Shakespeare is that, in a context in which Order is implied and advertised, we experience chaos and nihilism. It is the grim Beckettian refusal to be hoodwinked by the gloss of life which lies at the heart of Shakespeare. It is that perception which connects up with our own cynicism, our own angst and our own sense of ineluctable tragedy that keeps him alive for us.

* * *

I am reliably informed that the two books one is likely to find in almost every American household are the Bible and the collected works of William Shakespeare. If the theory that King James the First hired Shakespeare to help translate the King James Version is true then Shakespeare could well be the author of both.

HOW TO
RAPE SHAKESPEARE

Lecture delivered by Marowitz at the Deutsche Shakespeare-Gesellschaft West in Bochum, Germany, 1987

It has always struck me as curious that no sooner does one begin to talk about Shakespeare than one finds oneself talking politics. Despite the fact that Shakespeare is universally admired, in some quarters even revered, there is no question that Shakespeare is a political issue, and like all political issues, prompts strong differences of opinion.

The Conservatives have perhaps the most vocal and solidly entrenched position in regard to Shakespeare. They want to 'preserve his integrity' — which usually means ensuring that the satisfactions they originally derived from the plays are faithfully duplicated each time they are performed. The Moderates or Middle-of-the-Roaders are prepared to accept a change of period or a shift in emphasis, so long as the basic structure and spirit remains in tact. The Radicals eagerly applaud new innovations — the startling reinterpretations which enable Shakespeare's work to deliver new sensations — whether significant or not — whether justifiable or not – the 'novelty of effect' being for them the *summum bonum*. And there is an even more extreme sect — even further left of center, a kind of Lunatic Fringe I suppose you could call them, and for them there are no limits to the transformations that can be made to the canon. Restructuring, juxtaposing, interlarding, collating one work with another, modern vernacular mixed with classical idiom, rock music copulating with Elizabethan madrigals, lazer imagery and computer technology freely commingling Star Wars with Wars of the Roses. These zealots would go to any lengths to shatter our reverence for these hallowed works.

Each of these factions finds in Shakespeare ample justification for their own position. As with the Bible, the Shakespearean scripture can be quoted to prove whatever propositions are being advocated at any given time and, as with politics, the values and temperament of the different parties are usually irreconcilable. And yet, despite these differences and incompatibilities, the thirty-seven plays remain the living source of all these passionate divisions. It is almost as if Shakespeare was the author of a kind of Universal Constitution and, for the last four centuries, everyone has been noisily interpreting it according to their own lights.

I must confess that some of the most contemptible people I have ever known have loved Shakespeare, and I have found them hard to take. It's like sharing your bed with bigots, junkies, and people with incurable halitosis. For many of them, Shakespeare confirms their most deeply held world-view. They believe the Christian Universe was memorialized in his work and, from his sentiments, they find it easy to justify their bourgeois smugness, their conventionality and traditional morality. For them, one sometimes feels as if Shakespeare wrote only so that his aphorisms could be inscribed on their calendars.

Some of the most imbecilic people I have ever met regularly burnt incense at the Bard's altar — transforming his works into philosophies or modes of conduct which strained one's credibility. Believing, for instance, that Hamlet was a grandiloquent justification for doing nothing — for being, as one person once put it to me, 'eloquently unemployed.' Or that Lear was really about the pitfalls of social security and the old-age pension — and that unless we began to take better care of our senior citizens, we would always be plagued by natural disasters and family dissolutions. One ditsy old lady who never went to bed without her First Folio at her side, believed that Shakespeare was simply the reincarnation of St. Mark — and she had proven through copious research that the Collected Works were merely the Gospel of Saint Mark in dramatic form. And when I was in the army, I had a commanding officer who believed that Shakespeare was the guiding spirit behind military technology and that, were he alive today, he'd be an outspoken advocate of nuclear warfare. "Why even his last words were belligerent and hawkish. 'Blessed be the man that spares these stones. And cursed be he that moves my bones'."

Well, you will say, there are cranks everywhere — in all fields. But what can one say about the weirdos in the Shakespeare Establishment itself; I mean the people who write learned treatises on "The Semiotic Significance of the Ass's Head in A Midsummer Night's Dream" or "The Probable Syllabus at Wittenberg University During Hamlet's Tenure". For all these people, Shakespeare is, as he is for me, a living presence and a constant stimulus. But it does make one stop and wonder whether

Shakespeare is really a kind of irresistible magnet only for the mad and deluded people of the world and perhaps, only those who claim to be impervious to his spell are entirely normal. I don't know, and I certainly don't mean to cast any aspersions on this respectable Shakespearean assembly — all of whom I am sure are perfectly sane and reasonable people — although to be frank, no research has been conducted that would conclusively establish that fact.

What I am going to describe is some of the work that I have conducted with the plays of William Shakespeare — both in London, on the Continent and in America — and conducted, I might add, as a practical director in the theatre and not as a critic or an academic although it is impossible to work as a director without employing criticism and drawing upon academic reserves. And indeed, in recent years, there have been many directors who couldn't have made a move without plundering the work of the academic community. Where would Tyrone Guthrie have been without Professor Ernest Jones or Clifford Williams, Peter Brook and Georgio Strehler without Jan Kott?

The first of these classical experiments took place in the mid-sixties when I was connected with Peter Brook and the Royal Shakespeare Company Experimental Group. We had been exploring the possibility of conveying theatrical meaning without relying on narrative. This was a time when there was a general dissatisfaction with 'the word' and everyone from John Cage to William Burroughs was extolling the virtues of chance, random factors, fragmentation and discontinuity. Would it be possible, Brook and I conjectured, to convey some of the nuances and insights which are to be found in HAMLET through a kind of cut-up of the work which entirely abandoned its sequential story-line; which transmitted the play in bits and pieces, the way glistening shards of glass catch the eye of a spectator in a mobile. And what would flashes from the play look like if seen from the vantage-point of the central character; that is to say distorted and exaggerated as they might appear to the mind of a highly pressured young man with neurotic tendencies suffering from delusions and hallucinations?

The result was a sixty minute collage stitched together from random sections of the play and wedged into an arbitrary structure — namely the soliloquy, "How all occasions do inform against me," the one that, perhaps more than any other, expresses Hamlet's schizoid character. More interesting than the reassembly of the work itself was the challenge it put to actors who usually worked according to the rules of Aristotelian unity — building their performances from beginning to middle to end. Here they were asked to swing drastically from a scene on the battlements to the Closet Scene, to the Play Scene, to the Court Scene; juxtaposing moments of pathos with low comedy, shuttling between lyricism and rhetoric, intrigue and satire. Nothing lasted for more than two or three minutes; no scene could develop to a logical conclusion because no sooner was one begun than it would be intersected by another; no sooner did a character present himself than he would be supplanted by another. The play, like a moving mosaic, continually contrasted rhythms, moods, characters and situations. And built into the exercise was not only the play itself, but the adapter's attitude to the play. Critical comment and intellectual asides also had to be dramatized — since the collective perception of the play over some 400 years was an inescapable factor in its performance.

When an early version was performed at the Akademie der Kunste, it was soundly thrashed by the Berlin critic Friedrich Luft, who took it to be a travesty of the original work. A large number of Berlin students rebutted Herr Luft's review and, in demonstrations outside the theatre, circulated broadsides against his notice. As is so often the case in the heat of such controversies, the production was defended for virtues it did not possess, and damned for faults which were the very features for which it had been assembled in the first place. And again, Shakespeare served to fan the flames of a political dispute — the Conservatives deploring the dismantling of the classical text, the radicals championing it in the name of some undefined esthetic reform. It became fashionable to say that if you already knew HAMLET, this was a fascinating recension which would provide a kind of salutary shock. But the fact is the collage was eventually played before thousands of people who had never read HAMLET or seen the film, and their impressions (derived from discussions after the performance) were as valid and often as knowledgeable as those of scholars and veteran theatregoers. Because, as I have always contended, there is a kind of cultural smear of HAMLET in our collective unconscious and we grow up knowing the play even if we have never read it, never seen the film or attended any stage performance. The 'myth' of the play is older than the play itself, and the play's survival in the modern imagination draws on the centrifugal myth on which it is based. And when one assembles a collage version of the play, or a discontinuous gambol through its themes and issues, that myth is reactivated.

I have to point out hastily that the collage was not intended to be a gratuitous stylistic exercise, a way of demonstrating methods of dramatic discontinuity and fragmentation. I held a very particular view of HAMLET. I loathed him and his values and despised what he stood for. His loquacious moralizing which was only a pretext for cowardice for inaction. His intellectualization of issues that cried out for the remedy of direct action; his posturing and empty theatrics; his egoistic delight in providing banal acting-tips to hardy old professionals such as the Player King; his hollow bombast in the Funeral Scene where, incensed by the sight of Laertes' genuine grief at his sister's death, he feels obliged to manufacture a passion of his own to try to equal it, failing miserably; his using Horatio as a captive audience in order to exaggerate his prowess on the sea voyage where he contemptibly arranges the liquidation of two gormless schoolfellows — just as previously, he blindly and impetuously dispatched Polonius in his mother's chamber believing it was the King but knowing full well it couldn't be as he had just left him at prayer a moment ago.

In short, for me, Hamlet personified the Paralyzed Liberal — the man who 'talks a good show' and has eloquent opinions about every subject under the sun but, when faced with a real challenge, merely wilts and wanes like the gutless piece of baloney he is. Without wishing to vent that animus against the received-perception of 'the vacillating Dane,' there would have been no point or purpose in the adaptation. Unconsciously, the jumble and anarchy of the work's structure was probably part of one's deep-seated prejudice against the character. Being unable to take a knife and cut up Hamlet himself one did the next best thing which was to take a scissors and cut up the play in which he had been enshrined. And here, once again, we are talking Shakespeare but really talking politics; for Hamlet has become a sacred cow to the Reactionaries. They adore his platitudes; they romanticize his sensitivity; his reluctance to commit violence — despite the fact that that violence, were it performed, would be an honorable response to the greater violence committed against the dead King and the state to which his son owes a powerful allegiance.

In A MACBETH, slightly intoxicated with the collage format I had devised, I again set out to chop the play into salient pieces. As with HAMLET, the action was visualized through the eyes of the central protagonist. This time, rather more appropriately, since one conceived Macbeth as the victim of a witchcraft-plot masterminded by his wife, Lady Macbeth, the chief witch of a coven that included the Three Witches — a conspiracy which was made visually apparent by costuming the witches as Lady Macbeth's ladies-in-waiting and having them always appear together. Macbeth, like Icarus, flys too close to the sun, aspires too high and so is damned for it. Macbeth, like Faustus, sells his soul for advancement and like the Doctor from Wittenberg, has to pay an infernal price. What more fitting a punishment than a wife whose body is inhabited by the very demons which swarm throughout this diabolical play and who, while pretending to be a staunch champion and loyal spouse, "commends the ingredience of Macbeth's "poisoned chalice to his own lips."

In this treatment, I was concerned, as many directors have been, with the peculiar knot of trinities that winds its way through the play: three witches; three murderers; three murders; hence, in this version, three personified aspects of Macbeth: the timorous, the imperious, the nefarious, and three separate actors to play them simultaneously — just as Lady Macbeth had her three infernal surrogates in the witches.

Viewed this way, the political, the moral, the Christian aspects of the play disappear replaced by the metaphysical, the amoral, the pre-Christian elements which, in my view, are more deeply embedded than the history inspired by the Gunpowder Plot, which several critics contend was the inspiration for the play. In a version which selects certain characteristics, others are necessarily ignored. There are many who contend it is outrageous to approach Macbeth without taking the historical context into account but there never has been a production of any Shakespearean play which delivers *all* the goods. Interpretation means you place emphasis on some things to the exclusion of others — that is why there can be hundreds of productions of the works without ever exhausting their infinite possibilities. It is mere carping to complain for example, that Orson Welles' voodoo production in the 1930s was an eccentric or partial view of the play. It was no more eccentric or partial than Joan Littlewood's version which set it in World War One or a recent Los Angeles production which placed it in a post-nuclear world with all vestiges of western civilization obliterated. Every production provides only a partial insight in respect to the material that supports its view.

TAMING OF THE SHREW, like MERCHANT OF VENICE, is a play that always left a nasty taste in the mouth. Women despised it because no matter how much irony one got into that last speech of Katherine's to the assembled wives, it always smacked of male chauvinism and marital subjugation. The play itself, shorn of the highjinks and slapstick which usually embroider it, is a detestable story about a woman who is brainwashed by a scheming adventurer as cruel as he is avaricious.

What are the principles of brainwashing? We know them well now from the Korean War, from Vietnam, from certain East European societies. To successfully brainwash someone you have to deprive them of sleep and nourishment, dislocate their moral balance and reorder their value-system and ultimately, their personality. To get them to believe that it is the sun when obviously it is the moon and vice verse; to accept the fact that they are worthless inferiors who ought to be grateful to their tormentors for their life and their sustenance. This is precisely what Petruchio does to Katherine from their wedding to the play's last scene where, in a kind of reenactment of the Moscow Trials of the 30s, he displays the haughty and independent creature we encountered at first now transformed into a tame and docile, domesticated lackey.

The only way successfully to present THE TAMING OF THE SHREW is to shut one's eye to its contemptible sub-text and treat the whole thing as a jolly charade. Of course, Katherine fancied Petruchio, and of course, the belligerent courtship is just proof of the fact opposites attract and that indeed, this couple was really made for one another. And if, through these permutations, you can invent a lot of comic business and outlandish minor characters, you might just get away with it. But if one peels away all those arbitrary layers of gaiety and subterfuge and looks at the fable naked and unadorned, one finds a play closer to THE DUCHESS OF MALFI than THE COMEDY OF ERRORS; a Gothick Tragedy rather than an Elizabethan comedy.

I first adapted this play about fifteen years ago — selecting the key scenes between Petruchio, Kate and Baptista as grim, humorless demonstrations of man's cruelty to woman. To add to the point of the treatment, I wrote a contemporary sub-plot of my own in which a young couple, loosely based on Lucentio and Bianca, meet and enter into a relationship which gradually deteriorates into psychological and physical violence. Just when it reaches its lowest point, the young couple decide to marry — since the magic ritual of marriage is still believed to be able to heal the psychic scars men inflict upon women and vice versa. No doubt, when their marriage begins to fall apart, they will have a baby to 'save the marriage — just as they married in the first place, to 'save the relationship'. The Shakespeare scenes were interlarded with the modern scenes, and each story progressed separately. Petruchio's heartless tyrannization of Katherine giving way to the young couple's quarrels, ego-kriegs and mutual psychological mayhem. At the end, when a pale and beaten Katherine is hauled forward to deliver her final recantation — "Fie, fie, unknit that threatening unkind brow, and dart not scornful glances from, those eyes, to wound they lord, thy king, thy governor," etc. — the young couple, now dressed in resplendent modern wedding attire, join Katherine and Petruchio in a wedding tableau which resolves both the period and the contemporary sections of the play.

In the first version, the contemporary scenes were simplex and repetitive of the Shakespeare scenes. We saw the young woman inflicting upon the young man, in a thinly-veiled psychological form, the same kind of torture that Petruchio inflicted upon Katherine. In the second version, there was a certain parity between the young lovers; both were equally guilty of destroying the relationship and each other. In the third version, something in the human and social fabric was made responsible for the havoc between the boy and the girl. And in the fourth version, performed in Los Angeles, the cruelty and self-destructiveness had no apparent source — it was just something sucked out of the atmosphere that men and women generate together. It inferred that all relationships, by their very nature, were destined to corrode because people invariably fell in love with figments of their imagination, figments then imposed upon luckless objects, male and female, that just happened to be by. It took four different versions to get it right but the matrix of all these versions was the grim and dark fable that burrowed underneath that woefully uneven comedy called THE TAMING OF THE SHREW — and despite the fact that original material was added, the themes and ideas were extrapolated from the words and ideas of William Shakespeare no matter how remote they seemed to be from his original work.

Nonsense, many of you will say — some quietly, some noisily. All you did was distort one of Shakespeare's perennial comedies and reduce it to the dimensions of a soap opera. I would probably not dispute that, saying only that soap opera has become an inescapable factor in contemporary life, which perhaps explains it great success on television. Most people I know live soap opera lives and communicate in soap opera dialogue. Further I would say, to combine the mundane and the classical is to create a combination almost as perfect as a hamburger and, to push the point even further, I would add: when a playwright like Shakespeare provides us with the meat, it is almost a contemporary imperative for us to add the fries, onions and relish. Our job is to retrace, rediscover, reconsider and re-angle the classics — not simply regurgitate them. 'I rethink therefore I am' — said Descartes or at least he should have. — But I am running ahead of myself as I have not as yet discussed that other obnoxious comedy THE MERCHANT OF VENICE.

It is difficult, almost impossible, to come to a play like THE MERCHANT OF VENICE, whose central character is an orthodox Jew, without bringing to it all one has learned and read about the Jews in the past 2000 years. It is difficult, almost impossible, to obliterate from the mind the last seventy-five years of Jewish history which includes European pogroms, the Nazi death camps, the rise of Jewish Nationalism and the Arab-Israeli conflicts. Of course, Shakespeare had no knowledge of any of these things and it is undeniable that none of these factors enter into THE MERCHANT OF VENICE — and yet, can they be excluded from the consciousness of a spectator attending the play? They can, I suppose, if one is prepared to put the contemporary sensibility to sleep and only fasten onto the fairy-tale elements of Shakespeare's play; if one is prepared to say of Shakespeare's Jew, as of Shakespeare's Moor, that he has no actual contemporary parallel; that a red-bewigged, comic-Jew has no real affinities with an Israeli businessman or a modern Hebraic scholar, just as an Elizabethan 'moor' has no particular affinity with a ghetto black. But it is a difficult thesis to sustain, because there is a cultural tendon that links all Jews with their history (even their history in Shakespeare plays) and all blacks with *their* antecedents — even the 'noble Moor' who, though he knows nothing of Sharpeville or American race-riots, is still subjected to Venetian racial prejudice and considered an 'outsider' in his society. Rather than indulge in those strenuous mental calisthenics which enable us to separate our contemporary consciousness from that of Shakespeare's, I prefer to yoke them together, despite their differences and seeming incompatibilities.

What had always irritated me most about THE MERCHANT was that contemptible trial scene in which Shylock is progressively humiliated, stripped of all property and dignity and sent packing from the courtroom; a forced convert, a disreputable father, a disenfranchised citizen, an unmasked villain. It was to try to remove those stains from his reputation that I decided to reorder THE MERCHANT.

So long as Antonio remained 'a good man,' Shylock must be a villain, and so I set about putting Antonio's character into question. By setting the action in Palestine during the period of the British

Mandate, one had a ready-made villain. The anti-Semitism engendered during this period was mainly the result of the policies of Clement Atlee's Middle East policy, which severely restricted immigration of Jerusalem, thereby forcing hundreds of thousands of escaping Jews to return to Europe. The man who seemed to personify these policies (quite unfairly in fact) was Ernest Bevin, Foreign Secretary at the time. By identifying Antonio with Bevin and the deadly policies of the Atlee government and by lining up Shylock with the Jewish nationalist cause, particularly its extremist factions such as the Irgun and the Stern Gang, one created a completely different moral balance between the opposing forces in the play. The Venetian capitalists and adventurers were transformed into British colonialists and the Jews into committed nationalists. (Shus, briefly mentioned by Shakespeare, was materialized as an outright terrorist and Tubal transformed into a kind of Zionist front-man.) Shylock himself retained a certain ambiguity, vigorously playing the caricature-Jew before Antonio, Bassanio and their Jew-baiting British cohorts, but becoming a cold, calculating Talmudic stoic when among his own people; a 'man with a mission' who knows he is most effective to his cause by not showing his true mettle, except when he holds the upper hand.

As a result of this restructuring of Shylock's character and thanks to sections lifted piecemeal from Christopher Marlowe's THE JEW OF MALTA, it became possible to arrive at that detestable trial scene and make it turn out very differently. After all the intolerable penalties, including a forced conversion, are heaped upon Shylock's head and when he seems closest to collapse, it was possible to reverse his fortunes by invading the court room with his own supporters, taking authority out of the hands of the British colonialists and placing it in the hands of Zionist guerrillas. This done, the path was cleared to 'alienate' Shylock's eloquent defense of his people: "Hath not a Jew eyes? Hath not a Jew hands, organs, dimensions, senses, affections, passions?" etc. The scheming British oppressors are annihilated by vengeful Jewish Nationalists come to the moneylender's defense not only because he is Jewish, but because he, like them, believes in a cause more honorable than partition. For the first time in Shakespearean history, Shylock emerges from the Trial Scene victorious, and The

Duke, Antonio, Bassanio and Portia, soundly rebuked.

Is this distortion? Of course it is! Is it taking liberties? Unquestionably! It involves rifling Marlowe to revise Shakespeare to satisfy the whims of an intruding director. I have heard these arguments for almost thirty years — and during all that time I observe that Shakespeare has been renewed, rekindled and rejuvenated by writers and directors with just such an intrusive frame of mind: Peter Stein, Georgio Strehler, Jean Vilar, Benno Besson, Peter Brook, Tom Stoppard, Edward Bond, Arnold Wesker, Lee Blessing, Botho Strauss, etc. etc. And what are all these revisionists intruding into, I ask myself — the Sacred Temple of Academic Purity that scholars, critics and teachers have attempted to construct around the canon to protect it from the incursions of contemporary thought. Conservatism is the deadliest force in the world of art; for it preserves old sensations at the expense of new ones. If the Elizabethans had been conservative about Kyd, Holinshed, Seneca, Whetstone, Boccaccio and Belleforest, we would never have had Shakespeare. If the early traditionalists had had their way, every Shakespearean production would have been a bloodless transplant from the page to the stage. Another argument with which one is constantly hammered is this: if you wish these plays to say things they never intended, why don't you leave Shakespeare alone and write your own plays? Why kibitz your own ideas through the forms and words set down by another writer? Of course, the assumption behind that question is that there is a clear-cut meaning to the works in question and that I, for whatever reasons, am ignoring or distorting it but, as I've already stated, I think this is a false assumption. No play possesses exclusivity of meaning, and the greater the play, the more meanings it is able to engender.

But the other and more pertinent answer to that question is that the theatre works best on the basis of surprise. On the crudest level, one sees this in thrillers and murder-mysteries, but suspense and revelation are as much a part of the work of Harold Pinter and Sam Shepard as they are of Agatha Christie. And with many works of Shakespeare, one has a ready-made anticipation on the part of the public. They arrive with fixed expectations as to what they are going to see when certain plays of Shakespeare are announced. They get what they expect and they expect what they have been *led* to expect and it is only when they *don't* get what they have been *led* to expect that they are on the threshold of having an experience. It is that cultural expectation that swirls in our brains before the curtains rise on works such as HAMLET, MACBETH, LEAR or MERCHANT OF VENICE, which makes it possible for theatregoers to 'have an experience' — to have one precisely because it is not the one they have been anticipating. Many of the works of Shakespeare, because they are so well-established, so often performed, so widely studied, provide the given circumstances for this salutary shock, and in a way that no new play possibly could do. As I've said elsewhere: an audience is often like the implacable face of a stopped clock which will resist all efforts to be wound to the correct time out of an obsessive desire to maintain the integrity of its broken mechanism. It should be no wonder that art must occasionally give it a good shake to get it ticking again.

Many of these arguments stem from received perceptions of the plays themselves and in this regard, I must say, the nineteenth-century essayists Charles Lamb and his sister Mary were in many ways a remarkable couple. They were able to read the plays of William Shakespeare and translate them into simple, unambiguous and definitive narratives. It's quite an amazing feat, when you stop to think of it; a definitive rendition of what a play is actually about. I know few critics who are able to achieve such succinctness. But of course, apart from being impressive, it is also highly suspect because the 'stories' of the plays need not at all be the tales Lamb found in them. There are a myriad of other tales from Shakespeare that could be hatched from precisely the same sources.

Take ROMEO AND JULIET, for example. Two impressionable teenagers, that are so oblivious of the political situation in their country they don't realize that by violating their sectarian allegiances, they are also threatening their own well-being. Rather than accept the arbitrary dictates of their belligerent elders, they forge an illegal liaison and attempt to outwit those forces conspiring to keep them apart. One allegedly perishes — causing the suicide of the other. To the very end, neither Romeo nor Juliet ever realize that it wasn't the stars that crossed their destiny, but human vindictiveness in the form of partisan politics. Which is why ROMEO AND JULIET is, to my mind, such a 'tragedy'.

The aforementioned MERCHANT OF VENICE because of its curious Judaeo-Christian undertones is a play that either can be reduced to a Venetian squabble between two merchants or expanded into a metaphysical fable with overwhelming religious significance. It could be a tale of a man who personifies the entire Jewish faith and who decides to castrate a Christian who is himself the symbolic personification of Jesus Christ.

Cutting off a pound of flesh "in what part of" Antonio's "body pleaseth" Shylock can easily be construed as a castration-threat — especially since the psychoanalysts have demonstrated that 'displacement from below to above' is a psychological commonplace. And since, at the end of the play, Antonio insists that Shylock become a Christian, it is not too far-fetched to assume that, in vengefully exacting the full letter of his bond, Shylock is demanding that the Christian who has defaulted symbolically become a Jew? Shylock's vengeance against the merchant is imbued with that same tooth-for-a-tooth-and-eye-for-an-eye justice which whips through the pages of the Old Testament, of which he, Shylock, is such a staunch advocate. And Antonio, who is so inexplicably melancholy in the first scenes of this play, is very Jesus-like in all the sufferings that befall him: stoically bearing both his friends' grief and his own; gentle, generous, uncomplaining, a loyal friend, a good and virtuous soul. Only once does he vent his spleen — and that is against Shylock when the merchant reminds him how he "rated him," "spat upon his Jewish gabardine," called him "misbeliever, cutthroat and dog." But is this indignation not merely a kind of echo of Jesus' fury against the money-changers whom, during the Passover service after toppling their tables and scattering their coins, he drove out of the temple? And wasn't Shakespeare himself influenced by the Passion Plays he must have seen as a boy in Stratford, and didn't those biblical antagonisms seep into the work of the mature playwright when he decided to depict a conflict between Christian and Jewish ethics. I do not say that Antonio is necessarily Jesus or Shylock *actually* stands for the

God of the Jews — but the conflict between the two men is fueled by differences that can be traced back to those alternative religions and their story told from that standpoint. — A theological tale from Shakespeare?

One could go on to spin the tale of Hamlet, the aging playboy with a weakness for amateur theatricals, who tosses away a kingdom simply to impress a public that no longer believes in his credibility. Or, if one fancied a somewhat more whimsical tale, the story of Fortinbras, the bitter son of a defeated Norwegian king who, wanting to take revenge against his enemies, decides to impersonate the Ghost of Hamlet's dead father and, in that guise, appears to the son of the murdered monarch. He then proceeds to subvert the newly-formed government of Claudius and, through spiritualistic provocations against the highly impressionable student from Wittenberg, instigates the harassment of the Queen, subversion of the state and the consequent murders of Rosencrantz, Guildenstern and Polonius — not to mention the suicide of Ophelia — all as an elaborate plot that paves the way for the Norwegian's own succession — by default — to the Danish throne. — A far-fetched fable from Shakespeare.

Although they might astonish Charles and Mary Lamb, these are only some of the 'tales from Shakespeare' that can be woven out of the incidents of the plays.

There are as many tellers-of-these-tales as there are readers, as there are spectators, as there are imaginations to respond to their given circumstances and the blocks of language that constitute them. And what makes these 'departures' possible, in one production after another, is the endlessly malleable material of William Shakespeare.

Certainly there are those that are enraged by such extrapolations and Variations, not to say distortions, of what they take to be Shakespeare's original meaning; those that contend that a masterpiece already contains a richness of contemporary parallels which, because they exist in the depth of the text and the breadth of the spectator's imagination, need not be tangibly translated on the stage. Indeed, they would contend that by making one particular parallel explicit, it robs the play of other, more implicit meanings.

This is a persuasive argument until one considers the very nature of stage production. For in the theatre, the task of actors and directors is to make a play concrete. To make specific choices about decor, costume, textual emphasis and thematic interpretation. In the theatre, one cannot put on the stage a kind of multi-faceted resonating-Chamber called 'a classic,' and allow all members of the public to draw their own conclusions from it. The artist proceeds from conclusions he has *already* drawn from his reading of the text. The demands of his profession insist that he choose certain ideas, images, and issues over other ideas, images and issues. Since there is no way to render Shakespeare in a pristine state (i.e., to 'let Shakespeare speak for himself'), since interpretation necessarily involves diluting Shakespeare's work by putting him through the strainer of actors', directors' and designers' imaginations, the search for parallels is an unavoidable part of the theatre-work. Therefore, the public is always receiving Shakespeare-plus or, as is more often the case, Shakespeare-minus but what it is never receiving is Shakespeare pure.

The overriding esthetic question today is what permutations and what contemporary insights can be fashioned from the body of work bequeathed us over 400 years of Shakespearean dramaturgy. The answer to that question may involve the smallest fraction of Shakespeare's original work — perhaps none of his language at all and only some of the ideas lurking beneath his stories and his themes. Or it might involve radical reorganization of his actual materials — scenes, speeches, characters that are unmistakably Shakespearean but now taken into other hands and put to other purposes. Or it may involve modifications, revisions and adjustments to works with which we are very familiar — perhaps in order to remove some of that familiarity or replace it with newly-minted ideas. Shakespeare's political spectrum is wide. It accommodates Conservatives, Moderates, Radicals, True Believers, Atheists; Anarchists, Nihilists etc. It is as multifarious as an Italian parliament, as divided as the German Bündestag. But what it must never become is the exclusive property of academics. I would make Shakespeare available to everyone — except the sclerotic traditionalists — those semiotic vampires whose passion is to suck him dry and index him out of existence. Fortunately, despite their assumed sense of ownership, Shakespeare does not belong to the Shakespeare Establishment — and so long as they can be kept at bay, there is hope for the future.

Over the years, our Shakespearean understanding has gone from text to sub-text to ur-text and has now reached the stage of pretext — that is, the point where the original texts are being used as paradigms for alternative versions of the text. What we all most profoundly want from Shakespeare is not the routine repetition of his words and imagery, but the Shakespearean Experience, and today, ironically, that can come only from dissolving the works into a new compound — that is, creating that sense of vicissitude, variety and intellectual vigor with which the author himself confronted the experience of the sixteenth and seventeenth centuries.

We need not be Shakespeare to duplicate the Shakespearean Experience, but we do have to find the artistic resources in ourselves to duplicate his impact; and to do this, we must cut the umbilical cord that ties us to his literary tradition. To create the Shakespearean Experience, we have to re-imagine his themes and reconstitute his fables. The real mystery is not really who he was or where he came from, but why we allow his influence to inhibit our conception of what we are capable of turning him into. His 'greatness' is nothing more than the sperm-bank from which we must spawn our own off-springs. I talked earlier about the myths embedded in his works, but the greatest myth of all is that we cannot transcend him. Once we kill that myth, we will have launched our own renaissance — one that, theatrically speaking, is long overdue.

I have talked here about raping Shakespeare and can now admit that that was a cheap, sensationalist device merely to catch your attention (for we know that academics and pedagogues are as susceptible to sexual temptation as their students.) But despite my base motives there is still some aptness in the title. For even as we acknowledge that rape is a desecration of human dignity and a crime demanding strict punishment, we must also acknowledge that for the rapist there is an element of pleasure in the act. I do not suggest that rape should be a social pastime like jogging or aerobics, but I would point out that when the object of the rape is dead, that is no longer rape but necrophilia. Raping Shakespeare's plays at least treats them like living objects; making love to them when they are lifeless and inert is, in my view, a much more contemptible crime.

* * *

Postscript:

This talk was delivered some fifteen years ago when certain issues regarding reinterpretation were more disputatious than they are today. If it feels overly defensive that's because, subtextually, it was responding to attacks that were current at the time. It contains certain ideas and takes certain positions that I, an older and presumably wiser man, might well disavow. If I heard such sentiments expressed today, I would probably recoil from both their impetuosity and hyperbole. But since I vividly remember the person who first voiced them and clearly recall the passions that inspired him, I must admit to a certain fondness for the fellow and even a grudging sympathy for some of his wilder beliefs. It is the tone that is off-putting. It is the sound of an irascible youth that cannot resist overstatement and tends to grate on one's nerves. But I find my abiding affection for his zeal, intemperate as it may be, almost — if not entirely — dissolves all rancor.

STILL ALIVE

An Autobiographical Essay by Jan Kott

Translated by Jadwiga Kosicka. Yale University Press

Reviewed for AMERICAN BOOK REVIEW by Charles Marowitz

The trajectory of most books is from the eye to the brain and then out some imperceptible pee-hole at the back of the head. Only occasionally does something that you read enter the bloodstream and become a permanent part of your metabolism. Those are books which become so permanently lodged in the mental archives that they remain on instant recall for the rest of your life. Jan Kott's STILL ALIVE is that kind of book for me. I read it, savouringly over four or five days, and when I'd finished, found scenes and situations recurring in my dreams. An analyst would be able to provide some astute reason why that was so. He could probably prove that it connected up with personal psychic preoccupations triggered by the depicted events, but a critic would have a simpler explanation. He would point out that, being vivid, subtle, graphic and profound, the book fleshed out a world that, although known in general terms, here achieved a specificity that made it ineradicably memorable.

The book documents, in a haphazard and discontinuous way, the life of a Polish intellectual and political activist who suffered through the terrors of the German occupation and the even more terrifying reign of terror unleashed by the Soviet occupation, emerging from all these catastrophes with a philosophic detachment bordering on The Absurd. Almost every horrific war-time event is flecked with elements of black comedy. The unbearable and the absurd are constantly in tandem. First-class chronicles of the past seventy years of European history have been churned out at an alarming rate, but I know of none that captures the deracination of those decades as well as this; none that gives you the palpable sensation of actually being in the midst of the carnage, displacement and hunger which characterized those tumultuous years. The book presumes to be nothing more than a souvenir of the past, but being peppered with irony and stewed in bemused contemplation, it gradually becomes a kind of *PARADISE LOST* with survival taking the place of both Heaven and Hell.

Throughout the book, Kott, a university professor who rapidly became involved in the Polish resistance, allows his mind to wander from period to period, person to person, anecdote to anecdote, and yet despite the discontinuity, a kind of thematic through-line asserts itself. As if memory, spreading like buckshot and independent of chronology, had a logic of its own.

There are innumerable Polish characters with long, unpronounceable Polish names — party-workers, poets, writers, apparatchiks — far too many to achieve any recognizable identity, but it doesn't matter. The landscape itself is vivid and the gist of all the roachlike characters that inhabit it illustrate the same themes: bureaucratic oppression, ubiquitous fear of disappearance or death, threatened imprisonment and obliteration by decree. People are constantly being arrested, tortured, murdered or committing suicide, and little by little, the sense of living in a besieged society where virtually everyone's life is poised on a knife's-edge, insinuates itself upon the reader. It suddenly, and powerfully, makes sense of all those hideous 2nd World War films where refugees and hostages were constantly being terrorized by jack-booted storm-troopers. It siphons all the cliches out of those cinematic representations of World War II and, in the Brechtian sense, 'alienates' it as if seen for the first time.

Kott, a Jew who managed to obtain false-papers to prevent his ethnicity from sealing his doom, races from one city to the next, always a step ahead of the Gestapo and the threat of imminent extinction. Miraculously, he survives the war only to be submerged in the mausoleum of Soviet-occupied Poland. Here, because of his Communist credentials, there is a temporary improvement in his status, but in the unpredictable political atmosphere of this post-war Stalinist society, revisionism and the unpredictable vicissitudes of political factionalism force him to develop survival-skills even greater than those acquired under the Nazis.

Ultimately, there is an escape to the West where, now a highly lauded Shakespeare scholar, he settles down in a university at Stony Brook, New York, but the reverberations of what he has lived through never entirely subside. They condition his outlook and permeate his world-view. For Kott, the world will always be a place where the status quo can, in an instant, do a backflip; where storm follows calm and order precipitates chaos. This is the quintessential European experience of the early 20th century and Kott not only describes it, he contains and exemplifies it.

The style of the book is casually devastating. Confronted with the most terrifying circumstances, the eyes in Kott's Punch-like visage narrow, a smile plays on his lips and the author immediately detaches himself from catastrophe and, in a widening long-shot, proceeds to objectify his experience. Like the Good Soldier Schweik, Kott has the ability to be enmeshed in the most harrowing incidents and emerge relatively unscathed, his good humor miraculously in tact.

In the last chapters, Kott describes with clinical precision and total lack of sentimentality, the five heart attacks which, each time, almost snuffed out his life. The metabolic terror that assaults his body is the biological equivalent of the totalitarianism which wreaked such havoc on his social self between the 1930s and the 1960s. The cardiac arrests emerge like the progeny of Stalin and Hitler, Gomulka and Jaruzrelski. They are just as irrational, just as menacing, just as impossible to counter or cope with. The clinical descriptions segue into limpid, utterly sensible contemplations that give the book its solid philosophical anchor.

What always made Kott such a distinctive critic was the way in which he was able to find in the classics, particularly Shakespeare, the living essence of contemporary forces. It was Kott more than anyone else who showed us the connection between historical totalitarianism and contemporary power-politics; how the Kings Annointed and the modern despots shared both the same ideologies and techniques of plunder; how the so-called 'Grand Mechanism' was hatched in the middle ages and acquired sophistication right up to the present. (Bosnia being the chilling, most immediate example of his thesis.) What STILL ALIVE does is to spell out the experiential base from which those theories were hatched. It was because Kott lived the kind of life that he did that he was able to have the insights he had. What made him an astute critic of Shakespeare was not reading and scholarship, but converted perceptions about life's cruelties and absurdities. That is what has always lifted Kott far above his critical colleagues. They were writing exegeses; he was extrapolating from personal traumas and tragedies.

A personal note:

I first met Kott in the early 60s in England but got to know him very well when he relocated to Santa Monica in the 80s. In my many meetings with him, I would always excavate that endlessly fertile mind for insights and perceptions about Shakespeare. We almost never alluded to his personal life — the subject of this book — and when I finished it, I found myself kicking myself for my obtuseness. Instead of discussing 'gender theories' or 'medieval pageantry', I should have been asking him about the Polish resistance movement, the claustrophobic reality of living under Nazi and Soviet occupation, of being displaced from one corner of Europe to another. Instead of learning first-hand about what was really vital in his life, I contented myself with critical *aperçus.* And so for me, STILL ALIVE served a double purpose. It opened up a dimension of the man that I virtually knew nothing about and, in so doing, has given me a Jan Kott who is now even more precious than he was before. Secondly, it took the abstractions and clichés of the war-years and translated them into vivid, unforgettable terms. What makes STILL ALIVE such a compelling read is that from his earliest days right through the rigors of the past sixty years, Kott has always been bristlingly, electrically, unquenchably 'alive' and it is the quality of that indigenous liveliness which — being *still alive* — confers such magnetism to this book.

SHAKESPEARE, OUR CONTEMPORARY displays the length and breadth of Jan Kott's intellect, but STILL ALIVE *is* a literary microcosm which contains the soul of the man.